SEARCHING FOR HOME

THE IMPACT OF WWII ON A HIDDEN CHILD

JOSEPH GOSLER

ISBN 13: 9789493056350 (ebook)
ISBN 13: 9789493056343 (paperback)

Cover design and author photo: Sheila Wolper

Publisher: Amsterdam Publishers

Library of Congress Registration Number TXu 2-177-773

PRAISE

Seventy-five years after Auschwitz was liberated, we continue to come upon new stories, unfathomable lived experiences. Joseph Gosler's book is an important and moving addition to the history of the holocaust, giving us the perspective and trauma of a child reared in a Dutch family with a Dutch mother, only to learn after the war that he belongs to another family and mother.

PEARL ABRAHAM

Author of *Animal Voices, Mineral Hum: Stories, American Taliban* and *The Seventh Beggar*.

* * *

A child's psychological and identity development are inevitably impacted by the various traumas endured during wartime. Gosler's psychologically nuanced account of his youth in Europe, Israel and then in the United States, is a riveting and beautiful story of resilience of the human spirit as he is separated and eventually reunified with his family of origin by the end of World War II.

While he bends he does not break, and he manages to ultimately find contentment in life through his family, work, music, basketball, and his many dogs.

As a child psychologist, I have not come across another book that better captures the psychological turmoil encountered by a Jewish child who is separated as an infant from his birth parents during World War II only to be given a new name and live with a non-Jewish family before being reunified years later. Gosler's road to psychological survival and recovery is unique and inspiring. I recommend this to professionals and laypersons alike.

ALEC L. MILLER, PsyD

Co-Founder and Clinical Director, Cognitive & Behavioral Consultants, LLP, Clinical Professor of Psychiatry and Behavioral Sciences, Montefiore Medical Center/Albert Einstein College of Medicine

* * *

Joseph Gosler's sensitive, affecting and beautifully written memoir belongs in the last chapter of the history of WWII. Yet, *Searching for Home* will be of equal importance in the annals of psychological studies on the subject of separating a small child from the only family he knows.

The Holocaust initiates Joseph Gosler's early distress, but it is the aftermath that perpetuates a lifetime of dislocation and trauma. Born in the Netherlands in July 1942, the serial uprooting starts in early infancy, when he is hidden from the Nazis by a loving adoptive family, the Dijkstras. But his ordeal occurs when he is returned to his war-scarred parents after the liberation. A succession of displacements resumes with his parents, first in Israel and then in the U.S., establishing a long-lasting rift between Joe and his parents and a perennial simmering rage. Each relocation heightens his sense of not belonging anywhere and his constant fear that "life can be snuffed out or diminished in a nanosecond."

Still, from an early age, Joe is determined not to be a victim. As he searches for a personal identity and a home, he is remarkably self-aware and brutally honest. It is this willingness to bare himself completely open that sets this memoir apart from many others.

RACHELLE GOLDSTEIN

Co-director, Hidden Child Foundation/ADL

* * *

This beautiful poignant memoir of a very young Jewish child hidden with a Christian family in Holland during the Holocaust powerfully draws the reader in, while giving important historical and psychological context to the lifelong emotional devastation experienced by many child Holocaust survivors. The author's inspiring journey of perseverance offers hope for redemption to others.

ISRAELA MEYERSTEIN, MSW

Author of *Bridge to Healing: Finding Strength to Cope with Illness* and *Miracle Nation: Seventy Stories about the Spirit of Israel.*

I would like to dedicate this book to Moeder and Vader Dijkstra, their daughters Anneke and Folie and their respective families.

Without Moeder and Vader's love and protection, I would not be alive today.

I would also like to dedicate this book to Sheila Wolper, my wonderful partner, without whom I would be totally impoverished.

CONTENTS

ACKNOWLEDGMENTS

This story would not have been written without the encouragement and editorial support of a number of people. My dear friend Richard Eldridge, who inspired me to write and to listen to the world around me. Rena Diana, whose insights and grammatical infusions helped to create a more fluid story. Ron Singer, who reminded me that "less is more" and to stay on point. Doctor Patricia Miller, who helped to structure the story and whose opinions I always cherish. Brian Burke who tenaciously reminded me that it's a hidden child story and to narrow my focus.

And as it is said, "...the last shall be the first", Sheila Wolper, who has spent countless hours reading and rereading the manuscript: focusing on themes, structure, grammar, rhythm and flow. This book would have been very different without her direct support.

PROLOGUE

The cobblestones were washed each morning

The streets, built for horse and buggy travel did not support modern times.

The advent of the automobile and airplane were symbols of this new age. The thick mist of the 1930s was lifting and with the depression fading, new hopes and new political roots were becoming more entrenched.

The cobblestones were washed each morning

The air was mired with optimism.

Children played in the streets while their parents rushed off to work.

Very few people took the time to look beyond their own gardens.

If they did, they disassociated themselves from what they saw and heard. The rise of Nazi power was evident everywhere: shops vandalized, books burnt, cemeteries and places of worship desecrated. People beaten in the street.

Few questioned these onslaughts against the Jews, feeling, *Why should we care, they are not like us!*

There was a myopic sense of trust and belief that things would work out, that this too would pass.

They wished for a future that was well managed, orderly, with a single culture and political vision, a vision that excluded me.

The cobblestones were washed each morning

The traffic in the streets was now a mixture of people rushing everywhere, a few automobiles and many trucks, soldiers and tanks.

At dusk, people would come home from work with their groceries, listen to the radio and because of curfews rarely went out at night.

Many Jews went into hiding.

They hid wherever they could: in closets, attics, haylofts, and forests, or they obtained false identity papers and blended in.

The Nazi boot was everywhere and you could not trust anyone.

Mistakes were fatal.

The cobblestones were washed each morning

The parade of Nazi boots is gone.

The war ended.

The trucks and tanks are gone and people rush into the streets to celebrate and forget.

They stand on the souls of the dead.

BACKGROUND

Holland is one of the most densely populated countries in the world, located in northwestern Europe with Germany and Belgium its closest neighbors. Half the country lies below sea level. Its topography is primarily flat with few forests no mountain ranges, and a few hills. Holland's preoccupation with orderliness, and its general tolerance towards foreigners made it an attractive country to which people could emigrate. During the Inquisition and much of the sixteenth century, Jews fled to Holland from Spain, Portugal and Belgium. Between the seventeenth and nineteenth centuries, due to pogroms in Poland, Russia and Germany, more Jews fled to Holland. These new arrivals were primarily working class and poor and included my great-great grandparents from Germany.

The Dutch Jews were concentrated in the large cities of Amsterdam, Rotterdam and The Hague. Although they lived in the Jewish sector, they were assimilated into Dutch society, felt like "Nederlanders" and spoke Dutch, unlike Jews from eastern Europe who mainly spoke Yiddish and lived more restrictively.

When Holland was invaded in May 1940, there were

approximately eight million people, including 140,000 Jews. Of the latter, there were many Jews who had come from Germany and Austria, and countries further east, within the previous seven years. The Dutch who had not experienced war for more than a century, were shocked when on May 10th the Nazi tanks rolled into Holland. Three days later the Queen fled to England and a day thereafter Holland was overrun by the German military. However, Hitler saw the Dutch as racially similar and decided that instead of the military, a civil administration should manage day-to-day affairs, and appointed Arthur Seyss-Inquart, the former chancellor of Austria, as the new head of this administration.

At first very little changed. Prominent Jews were asked to meet with the mayor of Amsterdam and were assured that no harm would come to the Dutch Jews. It was too early in the war to know what was going to happen. In fact, the Nazis methodically kept such information from filtering into Holland and everyday life. They were so thorough that it was difficult for individuals who would later round up the Jews and escort them to Westerbork (a transition camp) or to Bergen-Belsen or any other concentration camps to know what atrocities took place in those camps. Basically, the Nazis were assessing whether the Dutch would resist before displaying their agenda.

However, by January 1941 their plans became very clear. All Dutch Jews had to register. A very efficient bureau as well as stiff penalties for non-compliance expedited the registration process. Dutch Jews prided themselves on being good citizens and practically every Jew registered, including my parents and extended family. By February of 1941, Jews needed to remain in their sectors, there were curfews and more than four hundred Jews were rounded up. Other groups were targeted as well: gypsies, homosexuals, the disabled, socialists and communists, but the "final solution" was meant for the Jews.

In support of the Jewish community, there was a general strike throughout Holland and for one day Holland stood still. In contrast to the support the Dutch people showed for Jews, Holland had the second largest Nazi party in Europe, the National Socialist Movement, known as the NSB. More than 100,000 Dutch people belonged to this far-right party, and with the support of Dutch sympathizers and the efficiency of the Dutch civil service, the Germans needed only a thousand Nazis to administer the country. Even the Jewish Council, which was made up of prominent Jews selected to keep order in the Jewish quarter, went well beyond what their Nazi supervisors required them to do.

An ongoing military presence was unnecessary in Holland because of the NSB. Instead, Holland was managed with the SS and their Dutch surrogates. This difference in infrastructure proved to be devastating for Dutch Jews, as illustrated by the fact that proportionately, there were fewer survivors in Holland than in any other western European country. Out of the 140,000 Dutch Jews, 110,000 were transported to various concentration camps and more than 25,000 went into hiding. Only 5,000 survived the camps and returned to Holland. Of those hidden, 17,000 returned from hiding. I was one of them.

INTRODUCTION

A baby cries for a multitude of reasons; the need for nourishment, warmth, nurturing, and comfort. As we grow, we learn to localize our thoughts and feelings, to broadcast who we are, and to claim space in the universe. It is these voices and stories that truly matter.

In my early twenty's, I saw a film about WW2 and one image in the film seared into my memory. A little boy in woolen shorts stands alone on a railway platform with a small suitcase by his side, crying, while people scurry about. The film's focus then shifts and follows the train as it leaves the station. The boy is not seen again. What happened to that little boy? The image, so raw in my mind, awakened feelings of fear, loss and longing that lay dormant since childhood. Once awakened they persisted like an anchor stunting my spirit and undermining my sense of self. All I could feel was rage!

Many years have passed and I have crossed the Rubicon, marching forward towards my final outpost. And yet, a recent event has forced me to slow down and reflect upon my life, from its very roots to the present time.

2018 began in a sad and sobering manner. For eleven years, I had a dog, a kindred spirit named Milton. A yellow Labrador Retriever with warm seal-like eyes who nurtured me as I nurtured him. He was a stereotypical lab with great temperament, energy, kindness, dependability, and so much more. He suddenly became ill and we found out that he had a form of stomach cancer. The weeks that followed were filled with struggle, pain, intense focus and prayer. But nothing worked and he died, as in life, staring into my eyes. I mourn him now as I mourn myself.

His eyes were portals into my past. Dogs have always been important to me. Not simply as playmates, confidants and living teddy bears, but as symbols of friendship and belonging. As a child growing up, my dogs were always waiting for me when I got home, ready to run after a ball or protect me from danger. They were also like faded markers along a winding road, reminding me of all the times we had to leave them behind, as our family moved from one country to another. Just as we could not take Whitey from Holland or Gura from Israel with us, I could not take my home, friends, school and neighborhood. Their loss was immediate and painful and crystalized my feelings of disorientation, insecurity and abandonment, as I lost everything that was familiar.

PART 1

THE NETHERLANDS
1942 - 1949

1

I was born on July 27th, 1942, to Henriette (Yetta) Swartberg-Gosler and Maurice Gosler in the northern provincial capital of Groningen. My mother tells me that it was a Monday morning, not distinguished by anything unusual except for the British bombers flying overhead, returning from their missions. My birth certificate notes the birth name of Joseph Gosler (named after my paternal grandfather) but my name changed numerous times during and after the war. Each new name represented a segment of my life, ever connected like the canals that crisscrossed my birth city of Groningen. Each experience and identity fused into another, shaping me into who I am today.

I began to walk early, a prophetic irony, because I wandered throughout my life searching for the place I belonged. But at this age, what would an infant know about what is to come? I had no conception of time and space, peek-a-boo was the new game in town, and the windowsill was still far out of my reach. The playpen was my castle, and my teddy bear a trusted companion. Some sunlight peered into the house, but the curtains were drawn to preserve the heavy dark furniture and rich brocade fabrics.

Unless the lights were on, the house was dark and somber, and seemed frozen in time. There was a small rectangular garden with a patch of grass, surrounded by a lush canopy of tulips, snow drops, hyacinth and honeysuckle. Some non-descript green bushes hid the fencing that separated our yard from our neighbor's.

My childhood home was one of many row houses with a flat red brick wall and chimney, dark green window trim and a recessed doorway, topped by a roof of jumbled orange slate shingles. Many entryways had colorful wall tiles and marble or slate steps. Our home, situated along the Kooijkerplein and sandwiched between Gorechtbuur and Oosterparkwijk, was a typical Dutch house that could have been located anywhere in the Netherlands.

My mother, thirty-five, grew up in the city of Assen. She was from an upper middle-class family with one sibling, her older brother, Leo. She believed herself to be a modern woman: enrolled in business courses after high school, studied to become a beautician, belonged to an athletic club, and was politically aware and socially active.

My father, thirty-two, came from Groningen, from a lower middle-class background. One of six siblings, he was stricken with polio as a child and lost hearing in his right ear. He left school in the eighth grade, became a butcher, and like my mother, belonged to an athletic club. Whether it was due to the polio or leaving school early, he was both timid and cautious when communicating with other people. It was common in those days for brothers and sisters to marry into one another's family. After the marriage of Leo, my mother's older brother to Maria, my father's older sister, my parents followed suit and married in 1941.

A month before my birth, The Nazi administration began the deportation of Jews, first to Westerbork and then to Bergen-Belsen or to the various eastern European concentration camps, like

Sobibor and Auschwitz. Although people were still employed, more and more limitations were set on Jews in terms of where they could work, where they could shop and when they could leave their homes. It became clear that if you wanted to survive, you had to leave the country or go into hiding.

The Resistance movement had just been formed and was in its embryonic stage. False identity papers were difficult to get. In retrospect, it seems strange to have a child during wartime, but I believe the Dutch including most Jews were determined to hold on to a sense of normalcy, even if it was forced. That was the odd part about life in Holland, at least through 1942, and since I never heard that my birth was accidental, I must assume that my parents felt secure enough to have me.

On the surface, my birth and infancy were no different than any other young child's. Except for the fact that we were Jews and unlike most Christian children, my father, Maurice, was arrested and sent to a forced labor camp near Kloosterveen at a time when my mother was seven months pregnant.

At the camp, he worked sixteen-hour days and had no means of escape. However, my mother sent him a letter, stating that she was ill, and asked if there was a way for him to come to her. Although the Nazi stranglehold on everyday life was becoming more formalized, here was an example of the schizophrenia of wartime Holland, because my father received a three-day pass. He visited us in August of 1942 when I was less than a month old.

After three days, ready to return to the camp, my mother noticed that the return date was omitted from his pass. My parents argued about this administrative error for hours. My father, ever true to his word, had every intention to keep his promise and return to the camp, until my mother convinced him otherwise. My father's typically Dutch sense of civic duty and honor that permeated all strata of society, would have cost him his life, if he had not been swayed by her words.

Fearing that the administration at Kloosterveen would follow up and find the omission, my parents and my widowed maternal grandmother left Groningen and travelled south to Amsterdam. The city had the largest Jewish quarter in Holland, and still held the promise of shelter, extended family and community.

Along the route, they mostly stayed on small family farms, never staying more than a single night, and usually leaving at dawn. They stayed away from train transportation for fear that they would become a focal point for questioning. Instead, they travelled in the countryside on foot, bicycle and local buses. The trip which normally took a few hours by train, took them four days.

The Jordaan or Jodenbuurt of Amsterdam was still a thriving quarter of nearly eighty thousand Jews. Many families could trace their family roots back to the 16th and 17th centuries. The Jews could worship and practice their religion without fear and live productive lives, which made the Netherlands and Amsterdam most specifically their new home. Though the Nazis had effectively changed the open-ended neighborhood into a ghetto, enforcing various restriction, mass deportations and the more extreme measures were still to come.

It was October 1942, and though life was more sobering it was still manageable. We found housing and my father found day labor. But, even as our days became predictable and routinized, my parents could tell that this was just a reprieve. The storm was near and more restrictions were placed on the ghetto.

The Jewish Council, serving as police, kept the community in-check, while the nightly Gestapo raids surgically removed any "troublemakers". It became crystal clear to my parents that they needed to remain mobile and flexible and that an infant undermined that possibility.

The new Dutch Resistance movement, although primarily engaged in intelligence gathering for the Allies, also had a special interest in saving Jewish children. Through friends, my parents contacted someone from the Resistance, and a plan and a rendezvous were devised.

2

At seven or eight months old, at an age when an infant can barely see beyond his mother's breast, I was taken from my parents by the Dutch Resistance to places unknown. One evening in March 1943, a nursing student on a bicycle with a straw basket attached came to our house, bundled me in a blanket, placed me in the basket and peddled off into the darkness.

Much later in my life my parents recounted their feelings of being in a state of controlled fear and numbness. Full of remorse and yet relieved, they hoped I would be safe, although there was no guarantee that they would ever see me again.

At the same time, though travelling with an elderly woman, they hoped their mobility would be less compromised without an infant. From time to time, they received tidbits of information about me, and once even a wrinkled photograph of me sitting next to a fat cat named Tobus, which they destroyed immediately. This was done for their protection as well as mine; they were never told where I was.

Though living in Amsterdam became progressively worse, with

deportations and nightly raids, my parents remained there for another three months. But each day became more difficult; informers were everywhere and work became harder to find. There were bounty hunters, the Dutch police and civil servants paid by the Nazis to ferret out the Jews and other undesirables. One of these bounty hunter groups, the Henneicke Column, tracked, found and delivered to the Nazis more than eight thousand Jews.

My parents and Oma, Martha, decided to travel to Gelderland, an agricultural province south east of Amsterdam. There, they hoped to work and hide on one of the many small farms which dotted the fertile plains. The distance between Amsterdam and Gelderland is less than fifty miles, and even by foot should not take more than two days to travel.

Each day, they travelled at dawn, each carrying valises filled with their meager belongings and keepsakes. They stayed off main roads and looked for shelter and food for the evening to come. The journey was particularly hard on my grandmother, who found it difficult to walk long distances.

One night, while sleeping in a small barn, my mother awoke convinced that their host had informed on them and told of their whereabouts to the SS police. The premonition meant that they had to leave immediately. My grandmother felt that she needed more time to rest and decided that she would meet them later that day.

Sadly, they never saw her again, and later learned that she was taken by the SS, deported and murdered in Sobibor. When I got older, I became painfully aware as had my parents, that intuition and timing could spell the difference between life and death, and that ironically, we were born under lucky stars.

3

My journey was much less turbulent than the journey of my parents and grandma. I was placed with Meneer and Mevrouw Dijkstra, a Christian Social Democratic family in Wageningen, a small city near the Rhine River, and by coincidence also in Gelderland.

My new family consisted of "Vader", a landscape architect, "Moeder", a housewife, and two daughters, Anneke and Folie, who were fourteen and eleven years old respectively. Both girls had straight blond hair and blue eyes, while I had wavy dark brown hair and hazel-green eyes.

Soon after my arrival, the Dijkstra's added me to their family register and I was now called Peter Dijkstra, or Pietje. Safe and content with the only family I knew, I cannot remember whether I missed my mother, or the familiarity of my parents' home, or the warmth of my mother's breast and voice, but my childhood with the Dijkstra's was as wholesome as wartime would allow.

The townspeople accepted the story the Dijkstra's told to explain my sudden appearance in the family. I was Pietje Dijkstra, the son of Moeder's sister, who had died soon after my birth.

The neighbors on Eekmolenweg most likely knew that the sudden appearance of this infant meant that he was Jewish, but no one betrayed the Dijkstra's. In fact, during the period of 1944-45, when food was scarce and foraging became a sobering competitive sport, one of these neighbors gave food ration cards to the Dijkstra family, knowing they had an extra child to feed. This is the paradox of war, it exaggerates the good and the bad. Examples of charity continually clashed with the mercenary greed of the Dutch collaborators.

The Dijkstra house, with its traditional orange slate roof, center chimney and weathered red brick walls had a small front yard and a rectangular backyard with a tree in its center. Through the dense brush that covered the backyard fencing you could see a concrete playground of an elementary school.

The house had a small dark living room with a piano and towards the back a kitchen and bathroom. Upstairs, there were three bedrooms and another bathroom. The cellar was a narrow, dank space, with peeling white paint. It became the hidden cave-like womb, where the Dijkstra family would rush when the Canadian bombers flew overhead.

The Dijkstra's had a cat named Tobus whom I followed constantly. Tobus, a grey tiger-striped male cat, was surprisingly well fed and almost as large as me. At first I held on to couch covers and chairs, as I wobbled my way towards him, but soon I became a steadier, more confident walker and wherever the well-fed Tobus went, so did l.

When Tobus climbed the tree in the backyard, I would try to follow, but he was much faster and more agile and I usually fell over, trying to keep up with him. At times the laughter and activity emanating from the playground were like a siren beckoning me.

Fixated and mesmerized, I would sit on the grass watching the children play in the schoolyard. Their laughter and games excited me and I wanted to join them.

I am told that I was two years old, when slowly, but determinedly I walked to town with Vader. We were going to the barbershop and I was excited about my first haircut, although I grimaced with fear when the barber approached. He was going to cut my hair which, after all, was part of my body.

But, when the first curls fell, like feathers drifting to the floor, I relaxed and enjoyed the sensation, until the rumbling sounds of tanks rolling over uneven cobblestones made me jerk my head to see what was happening outside.

The smells and sounds of diesel-fed trucks and the rhythmic thud of leather boots made everyone in the shop turn towards the street. Suddenly I yelled, "Rotmoffen!" Hands came flying from every direction to cup my mouth and drag me to the back room. I was innocently mimicking what Moeder and Vader said in the quiet of their home about the occupiers when they marched past our home.

The men in the barbershop were much relieved when the parade of helmets and leather boots marched on in their robot-like rhythm without coming to a halt. Yelling "rotten Nazis", even by a child of two could mean death.

Some neighbors knew I was Jewish and this knowledge frightened Moeder and Vader. They were very careful to make sure that neither Anneke nor Folie would accidentally tell Pietje's true story to one of their friends. Danger, however, was prevalent through betrayal, or simply by playing outside.

One day, while playing with other young children in the street, a platoon of Nazi soldiers and tanks, came rolling down the street. All the other children scampered to the sides, but whether numb, curious, dumb or defiant, I remained in the middle of the road. The other children yelled for me to move to one side or the other, but I stood frozen.

Miraculously, the troops with their armaments divided from one stream into two as they passed me by. Moeder witnessed all of this from the front yard, and when she ran to retrieve me, they had already passed. These were perilous times, but for me from my two-year-old eyes it was part of the everyday experience.

It was now 1944. On the eastern front the Red Army and a particularly harsh winter combined to freeze the Nazi machine in its tracks. Simultaneously Canadian forces were nearing the Rhine River from the west. Food was scarce, and the Canadian bombing flights meant that we were spending more and more time in our tiny cellar.

During those hours I sat pensively on Moeder's lap, while Anneke and Folie sat between her and Vader. We wore several layers of clothing to ward off the damp cold. A single overhead light bulb flickered, but surprisingly remained lit for long periods of time. Books were read, songs were sung, and the collective hum of airplane engines overhead fused together to create white noise that lulled me to sleep.

The winter months were especially brutal. Even the root vegetables, potatoes, carrots and beets that were normally plentiful were scarce in the market place. There were acts of sabotage by the Resistance, vandalism for food was rampant and allied bombing became a nightly event.

These sobering events, however, did not deter me from my daily adventures in our backyard. I finally found a small opening in the chain-link fence that separated our backyard from the schoolyard.

One day, without Anneke or Moeder knowing, I crawled through the small opening that was near the ground and triumphantly made my way into the schoolyard. Tentative at first, I watched the older kids at play, but soon wandered closer. A girl, with short brown hair and a red bow on the right side of her head, saw me first and soon a gaggle of kids surrounded me. Although it was winter I wore short woolen pants, high socks, a thick sweater that covered other layers and a woolen cap that covered my ears. I clearly enjoyed the attention, but the sudden gathering caught the attention of several teachers who were standing nearby. I was swiftly escorted back to the fence and they bore witness as I slowly made my way back to our backyard.

It was a little secret I kept to myself, and I never tried crawling through the fence again. Whether it was simply the curiosity of a two-and-a-half-year-old or a yearning to wander, to touch other people, to communicate with the world around me or to search for what was missing, this need continued to be central to me throughout my life.

It wasn't long after my secret adventure that my underground family began to pack valises and trunks. The intention was to go further north, to Moeder's family, who lived on a farm in Friesland. Nestled in the countryside we would be away from the bombing, the harshness of daily life and the fear of betrayal.

During the hectic week before we travelled north, suddenly a knock was heard at the door, and without response, a Nazi soldier walked in. It was quite cold outside, and he asked Moeder to make him some tea.

I was playing with some finger puppets on the floor, and tentatively made my way to the table where the soldier sat. Inquisitively, I looked at the soldier and he smiled at me, simultaneously putting his heavy helmet on my head. The suddenness of the event startled me and I began to cry. I don't know why I cried, whether I was simply startled, angry, or just uncomfortable, but it prompted Moeder to come back from the kitchen. The awkwardness was palpable and the soldier picked up his helmet and left the house without drinking his tea. We left for Friesland and Oom Herman's farm the following morning.

Oom Herman's chicken farm was in Noord Bergum. He and his wife, Anne, owned a small farm on five hectares (12 acres) of land. Although they rarely had meat or dairy to sell in the market place, surprisingly they had enough food for themselves, and were happy to share with the Dijkstra family from Wageningen.

The farm had a few milking cows, a very large old female pig, a number of chickens (layers), one rooster, two geese, and no children prior to our arrival. The pig, who was named Marta, was more of a watch dog, in lieu of not having one.

Oom Herman, perhaps unaccustomed to children, or concerned about harboring a Jewish child, kept a watchful eye on me. Wherever I went and whatever I did, Herman followed. But, not quite three, I was a ball of energy, curiosity, and mischief, and it came as no surprise that he couldn't keep up with me.

The Dutch are often stereotyped as being stingy and pragmatic, fixated by routines and the guardians of clean sidewalks. Oom Herman was the quintessential Dutchman and he never wavered from his daily routine. Each morning he would put on his long johns, followed by thick black corduroy pants, two pairs of woolen socks, his *klompen* (wooden shoes), a thick flannel shirt and a jacket to begin his day milking the cows in the barn.

On one such occasion, I watched him dutifully milk each cow and pour the milk out of the bucket into a large stainless steel vat. He would repeat this ritual two or three times per day. Herman skimmed off the cream that rose to the top of the unpasteurized milk and put it into a smaller stainless pitcher. The cream was used for making whipped cream and cheese, added to soups, stews and strong coffee.

One morning when Herman checked his thirty-gallon milk vat, he noticed some grasses floating on top and some mud-colored streaks crisscrossing the white milk.

I had decided to mimic Herman's milking process just as I pretended to do what Moeder and Tante Anne would do when cooking the evening meal. Only this time, I simply added my version of herbs and spices. and with a long stick stirred the vat to and fro. Oom Herman was livid.

As punishment and to ensure that I didn't create further havoc, he tied me to a large Sycamore maple tree. The rope felt tight and was wrapped around the base of the tree. At first I was embarrassed and dumbfounded, but then focused on the challenge in front of me. I struggled for a while until I realized that if I took off my bulky clothes, I would be able to slip out of the ropes that kept me tied. Ten minutes later, I was scot-free and buck naked, running around like a young colt. I think everyone including Oom Herman had a good laugh, then quickly took me inside before I caught the grippe.

4

While my life seemed relatively normal, my parents, who were also in hiding, were not as fortunate, even though they had false identity papers. My mother, Yetta, was now "Dina Elisabeth Buttikhuis" and my father, Maurice, was "Sijbe Wjaarda".

My mother was a small woman, about five feet tall with brown hair and thick glasses. Behind her glasses were grey-blue eyes and wispy eyebrows, surrounded by white soft skin, and thin lips. A slightly pink mole on the left side of her chin lay just below the crease of her smile. Her nose was prominent, but straight and her large ears were, fortunately, hidden under her brown hair. Her facial characteristics suggested that she was not of Jewish descent and this allowed her a margin of safety.

On the other hand, my father or "Sijbe", was small and muscular, nearly bald, and what hair was left, was dark and almost kinky. His large brown eyes, full lips and skin that tanned quickly during the summer, betrayed Judaic ancestry.

Sijbe worked in an institution for the insane in Rekken (Gelderland), while Dina lived on a farm nearby. Between late

27

1944 and early 1945 as the Nazis began their retreat, life became even more precarious and they moved from one farm to another in the towns of Hengelo, De Heurne and Zelhem.

Their luck ran out when they were arrested in Doetinchem in March 1945. My father was sent to Westerbork the following day, while my mother—believed to be a Christian—was beaten for living with a Jew. She received a stern warning that if she were caught associating with a Jew again, she would be killed.

It was now the beginning of spring, 1945, and in the south of Holland, near Maastricht, the fighting had ceased and the people were free to walk the streets. It would take many weeks, until May 11, before the rest of Holland was freed. The streets were teaming with people. Relief, joy and pain were clearly etched on the Dutch faces.

The Jews, who returned from the camps or resurfaced from hiding, were psychologically gutted and physically damaged, sometimes beyond recognition. They searched for their loved ones, their friends, and old homes. They wanted to reconnect, as well as to forget.

There was chaos in the courts. Jewish children, like chattel, were tugged and pulled in one direction or another. A relative would make a claim for a cousin, nephew or niece, while his underground Christian parents would not give up the child they had grown to love. Or, on the other hand the court would allow the relative to adopt only to find out thereafter that the child was abused by that relative, or that the child wanted to return to her Christian parents.

There were also many Christian families who dutifully, though with definite remorse, returned the Jewish children in their care to their returning biological parent(s) or relative(s). Property restitution suits regarding homes, paintings and other valuables, log jammed the legal system.

It was a period of euphoria. For some, a period of hysteria and for others, of hate and vengeance. These were fluid times, and many victims felt all of these emotions simultaneously.

The Dutch collaborators, the police, civil servants and other Nazi supporters as well as the NSB and the Dutch civilians who fought for the Germans, had all disappeared. Many were later identified and brought to trial, but few received the punishment they truly deserved. The NSB was outlawed as a political party and no longer had any representatives in the Dutch parliament. Added to this emotional and physical turmoil, the economy was in shambles.

5

It took weeks before Yetta knew whether Maurice was alive. After he made his way back to Gelderland on a bicycle with wooden wheels, they reunited.

The two months at Westerbork had taken its toll on him. His feet were bleeding, his lower back was debilitated and he had lost 35% of his body weight. The stress and hopelessness he felt and the oppressive labor, left him gaunt and listless. The abuse and slave labor crushed his heart and spirit.

He was a cardboard image of his former self. But at least they were together again and Yetta was ten weeks pregnant, with my sister, Marja.

It took them another four weeks to search the underground records to find me and to finish the legal paperwork before they could embrace the child they had given away.

6

Nearly three years had passed. The infant they remembered had not only physically changed but, emotionally and psychologically had wrapped himself in the arms of the Dijkstra family. My parents were strangers. I did not recognize them, and wanted to return to Moeder and Vader. At age three I was confused and angered by the loss of my underground family.

I do know that many years later, when I began to thaw and connect with the swirl of emotions that welled within me, that my subterraneous outbursts which surfaced without warning, were fueled by a deep sense of abandonment.

We were back together again, but each member was irrevocably damaged by the experience of war. We returned to Groningen. My parents were devastated by the loss of their family: parents, brothers, sisters, aunts, uncles, and cousins. They also lost their homes, jobs, careers, friends and—more importantly—their spirit.

Every street had a story to tell. If the cobble stones could talk, you would hear the screams, moans and whispers of those who remained and those who were taken away. Every day was consumed by painful memories. My parents were in an endless state of mourning. They seemed to have aged well beyond their years.

At three years old, I was still wrapped in innocence, but cracks were beginning to form in my porcelain psyche. Although reunited with my biological parents, I felt abandoned by the only family I had known. I cried for Moeder. I was angry, anxious and confused. I trusted no one.

The war ravaged us all in so many ways. In early summer, my mother suffered a nervous breakdown. The feelings she held in so valiantly during the war, tied up in neat, little, locked boxes, now burst out and she was overwhelmed by sadness and rage. She barely functioned; her mind was elsewhere and her spirit was not to be found. She loved her children, but could not fully nurture them, since she could barely nurture herself.

My father, emotionally void, could not tend to her either, because he was desperately seeking work. My parents were so needy and self-absorbed, that the normal bonding between child and parent did not occur for me until much later in life. It is also possible that my longing for Moeder and Vader and my inability to forgive my own parents, delayed the bonding even more.

Thereafter, still struggling with severe depression and fatigue, my mother experienced the movements within her. Life forming inside her, and the healing grace of time itself, helped her regain some emotional footing, instilling a sense of harmony and rhythm to her daily life. My father found a job as an electrical appliance salesman. There was now a semblance of order in the home.

I did not know it at the time, but for me the cracks in my psyche were ever more apparent. What could a three-year-old know about the lasting effects of being a hidden child. For that matter, what could anyone know. I was disoriented and could not understand or accept why I was separated from Moeder and Vader.

Within weeks after I was reunited with my parents, I found a box of matches and promptly set the bathroom window curtains on fire. Naturally, my parents were alarmed, but this was not a time when adults were psychologically attuned. They did not understand it as a cry for help, an outward expression of my inner anguish, and my way of displaying rage, and my longing for Moeder and Vader.

In my heart, I was still Pietje Dijkstra and I wanted to go home. I yearned for my other life. Years later, I learned from my cousin Judith, that she would tease me about my name all the time. She would say, "Your name is Josje Gosler." And I would say, with great anger, "No! My name is Pietje Dijkstra!"

Was it a coincidence or a sense of guilt for being preoccupied with my newborn sister, Marja, that prompted my parents to buy a little white Spaniel-mix puppy? I do not know. The puppy had two black patches, one on its right side and the other around its left eye. We called him Whitey and he and I bonded immediately.

Wherever Whitey went, I would follow, and wherever I went, he followed dutifully. Our souls seemed to meld into one another, eye contact was all we needed to validate the feelings and thoughts we shared.

Whitey was the first of many dogs to follow, who helped me gain a semblance of stability, who comforted and nurtured me and who shared in my experience. No words could fully capture the loss I felt whenever, reluctantly, my family moved and left my dog behind. Each time it happened, another scar formed on my fragile psyche. The pain was pervasive, cumulative and remained raw.

Within a year's time, Whitey came up to my knee and would almost knock me over when he jumped up and pressed his front paws on my small chest. Strangely, Whitey grounded me, and enabled me to form attachments and to make friends.

It was with this newfound confidence that I became more

adventurous and began to make little forays beyond the front door of our house. I was four and a half years old and knew my address by heart: 77 Peter Hendrikstraat.

These adventures would infuse me with excitement and wonder. The country was full swing into reconstruction and eager to hide the physical scars of war. The sounds of demolition, the cleaning of debris, the new construction, and the cadres of military men that passed by, mesmerized me. I could not help but follow.

It was on one such occasion that I saw a group of sailors walking by, followed by a few jeeps and trucks. I was dazzled by their uniforms and rifles, and asked where they were going. They told me they were going towards the beaches to look for live mines. I asked one sailor if I could have a rifle, and he promised to bring me one when they returned. I followed them for a while, and then for a while longer, but lost sight of them as their stride was so much faster than mine.

I had never walked this far before (to downtown Groningen), and I marveled at the big buildings in front of me. Little did I know that I stood in front of the Stadhuis (townhall) in the Grote Markt, the very building that was used by the Nazis as their northern central command during the War.

To me it felt as though I had been out all day, but in fact it was only an hour, and so I rushed back to 77 Peter Hendrikstraat, well before anyone knew I was gone. In those days, it was common for young children to play in front of their homes unsupervised. There were few automobiles, and the idea of being kidnapped was unheard of.

Weather permitting, mommy would often spend early afternoons in front of the house, seated on a chair, doing some knitting, or reading a newspaper, while my sister, as a sixteen-month toddler, napped in a sturdy baby carriage. The sun was comforting and the leisure pace of life outside was still more stimulating than being cooped up in the house all day. I was kicking a small soccer ball and trying to mimic the various moves made by the older boys playing football. While this was happening, mommy went inside to make herself a cup of tea.

No more than ten minutes had elapsed when she returned to her chair. But, neither I nor the carriage, were to be found, only the white ball remained. She anxiously looked down each side of the street, but we were not to be seen. She didn't know which way to turn and asked the older boys at play, but they had not paid attention to anything but their game. She frantically proceeded to ask neighbors and strangers on the street if they had seen her children.

This is how she found out that a little boy was seen pushing a carriage down the street, going towards downtown Groningen. She rushed in that direction and could see me dutifully pushing the carriage, carefully watching cars and trolleys, as I made my way.

I do not know whether I was running away with my sister to find Moeder and Vader or simply wanted to share my big adventure to the Grote Markt with her, but that was not to be. Instead, I got a spanking, followed by a warm hug, before mommy took us home.

The family gained some normalcy, poppy had a job and mommy tended to us. Marja was nearly two and I made friends with Dimo, a boy who lived nearby.

Yet, my restlessness persisted and though I no longer wandered off as much, it still surfaced, fortunately in a less dramatic fashion. I felt stuck, controlled, and possibly still exposed to danger. Even when mommy made soup for dinner, I could not wait for it to cool down. Instead, I would go out and walk around the block and by the time I came back, the soup was just right.

At our home in Groningen, Marja and I would play together, like many siblings, though at this age of two and five respectively, it was more that I would play and Marja would watch. Her freckled round face and green eyes would shine, as she embraced the spectacle of puppets, voices and music. The potbelly stove was not in use during the summer, and was a perfect height to hold a small puppet theater stage.

At the time, I liked playing with finger and hand puppets, using different voices to personify different emotions, and characters. Marja was a great audience. But she was more than that, she filled part of the emptiness that I felt. Guiding her, and being the "big" brother, gave me stature and meaning, which helped counterbalance the distance I felt towards my parents. A separation I could not understand. A distance they could never seem to reduce.

She loved to watch me perform, and laughed with delight at my puppets' antics. But, once the performance didn't go as planned. Suddenly, the lid of the stove slid towards Marja, hitting her just above the eye. Her screams startled me and brought mommy into the room. It was several months before I had another puppet show, with Marja at a safe distance, her forehead distinguished by a one-inch scar just above her eye.

It was nearing December 5th and I always looked forward to Christmas or *Kerst* and the festivities in the square near the Martini Kerk (church). It was there that Christmas songs were sung, Punch and Judy puppet shows would hypnotize the gathered crowd, and Sinterklaas and Zwarte Piet would appear and hand out gifts to the children. One song that I and other children sang was:

DUTCH
"Sinterklaas Kapoentje,
Gooi wat in mijn schoentje,
Gooi wat in mijn laarsje,
Dank u Sinterklaasje!"

ENGLISH
"Saint Nicholas, Little Rascal,
Put something into my little shoe,
Put something into my little boot,
Thank you, little Saint Nicholas!"

Unlike the roly-poly Santa known in the United States, Sinterklaas was portrayed as a medieval saint, usually tall, thin and white bearded. Folklore has it that he came by boat from Spain, and sat at the helm of the boat with his long staff. Zwarte Piet was an African servant or "little helper", also dressed in medieval jester garb.

As a child, I couldn't wait for this annual spectacle; I didn't realize how racist it was until I became an adult. The idea and character of Zwarte Piet is demeaning and insulting and is now being altered in the Netherlands, but nostalgia and tradition stand rigidly in the way.

Unbeknown to Marja and me, mommy and poppy were planning to move. The post-war economy in the Netherlands had not rebounded. More than sixty percent of the railways were still in disrepair and Holland was functioning on a production level that was one third of their capacity as compared to pre-war levels. Food rationing still existed and if it weren't for the Marshall Plan in the late 1940s and 50s, it would have taken the country and all of Europe even longer to recover.

My father was dissatisfied with his job, and the nightmares of the war were ever present. They needed to distance themselves from the streets, shops, people, and most importantly the memories that continued to haunt them.

They attempted to get visas for America, but applied very late in the process. It was difficult, if not impossible to find a "host" in America who would sponsor us. Some of our relatives had applied earlier and were lucky to secure hosts, but our parents were not so fortunate.

It would be years before visas to America could be secured and our parents were desperate to leave. On the other hand, Israel was in its first year of existence and was eager to embrace new arrivals.

After months and months of planning, packing and a series of goodbyes to a small group of family and friends who also survived the war, the Gosler family waved their final goodbye and boarded the train for Marseille, France.

Once again, I was displaced, separated from all that was "home" and security. I had to leave Whitey and Dimo behind. How could I find my way, the road back was so dark, the road forward unclear, and in between them no foundation for trust?

PART 2
ISRAEL 1949 - 1953

7

The train rides from Groningen to Amsterdam and then from Amsterdam to Marseille were pleasantly uneventful. There was more than one Gosler family that boarded the train in Groningen that day. Jules was my father's older brother, oldest of six siblings, and he, and his wife, Emmy, and their daughter, Marion, were also traveling to Israel.

To me, at age six the train ride was a blur, but my memory of the ship voyage from Marseille was another matter. We traveled on a cargo ship bound for Haifa.

The passengers, like us, were Jewish Holocaust survivors. We slept in steerage, an open space in the bottom of the ship, where we were packed in with many other families, metal beds, suitcases, and buckets. There was always a long line for the single bathroom.

The trip took five days and the memory of a single stormy night is etched in my mind. The storm jolted the normal chaos into a horrific scene that lasted for several hours. Suitcases slid from one side of steerage to the other, buckets of urine spilled across the floor, beds rattled like chattering teeth, and babies cried incessantly as the flickering lights created a haunting disco light show.

In retrospect, I cannot imagine the humiliation they felt, the lack of privacy, the pervasive and lingering odors, coupled with the cries of infants. How different was it from the atmosphere in the cattle cars going to the camps?

We arrived the following day in the port of Haifa, relieved that the crossing had shifted from a night of darkness, turbulence, and fear into daylight, with the calm, warm breezes of Haifa's harbor symbolic of the hope for a new beginning. We were going to the promised land.

In those days, immigrants had no choice about where they would live or what they would do, unless you possessed rare skills or talents, or knew higher-ups in the government.

Both Gosler households were first placed in a transition camp, consisting of large sturdy canvas tents, outhouses and areas where water spigots were located. It was at this location that evaluations were made in terms of whether the adults would qualify to serve in the army and what kibbutz they could best serve.

In 1949, Kibbutzim were the backbone of Israel's economy. It also fostered the social fabric and nurtured the young spirit of this newly developed country. Although the cities of Jerusalem, Haifa, and Tel Aviv / Jaffa were in existence for a long time, the heart of young Israel was the kibbutz.

I don't recall the number of months we spent at this transition camp, but I do recall that my father worked as a cook for the army, and clandestinely, would smuggle butter and jam and some other goodies home. We stayed a short while at the camp, before both Gosler families were directed to live and work in Beit HaShita, a kibbutz in the northern part of the country.

Beit HaShita (House of Acacia) was located between the cities of

Afula and Beit She'an, a stone's throw from the Gilboa mountain range that runs from the West Bank and duly north-west. Beit HaShita, was one of the older kibbutzim, having been established at its current site in 1934.

Like many other kibbutzim at that time, it was Zionist and secular, and by 1949, had embraced a left wing, Socialist (Mapam) political philosophy. Nearby was the Arab village of Shatta, and the early Zionist settlers purchased land from them at well below market prices.

The villagers who did not want to sell their land, were evicted from their homes. A granddaughter of an early settler, Jasmine Donahaye, wrote *Losing Israel* about the Arab evictions. More land was taken after the War for Independence when Beit HaShita took the land near Yubla.

By the time the two Gosler families arrived, there were approximately six hundred settlers there, which was considered large at the time. The kibbutz had a herd of cows, many chickens and they even stocked fish. They produced cotton, wheat, melons, olives and citrus fruit.

8

We were not prepared for kibbutz life, and we each experienced it very differently. The separation of children from their parents, a heavenly reality for me, was a form of purgatory for my parents and sister.

I craved the distance from my parents, the independence to roam, and the camaraderie of children my age. The distance from my parents allowed me the profound space to sort things out and to begin to understand who I was. I felt totally smothered, bewildered, and resistant to my parents' attention, and unknowingly still mourned my own losses. The kibbutz was a perfect haven.

On the other hand, my parents and sister found it difficult to adapt to the kibbutz. The traditional family unit so ingrained in their consciousness, was disrupted and everything they used or wore was communally shared.

Marja's experience contrasted sharply with mine. She was quite sick when we first arrived at the placement camp in 1949, with a severe case of diarrhea that was exacerbated by the unsanitary conditions experienced on the cargo ship.

By the time we reached the placement camp, she had dysentery, and could have died. She was nearly three when we came to the kibbutz and—like all children—she lived in the dorms.

While I needed distance from my parents, Marja's needs were just the opposite. Even in Holland, Marja intuited that our mother was emotionally fragile and self-absorbed, and she felt neglected. At least a few evenings per week, for quite a while, she made her way to our parent's cottage and would wake up sleeping in their bed.

As she grew older, she became more independent, so much so that at age five she was hitchhiking and wandering by herself along the main road outside Beit HaShita.

This sense of independence, that I also shared, was very much the result of living on the kibbutz. Experiencing relationships beyond the nuclear family, as in a kibbutz, was as much a transition of emotional connectedness as it was a shift in one's political consciousness. No longer was the traditional home and family the only place of safety, the kibbutz and the surrounding community were as well.

My father, Maurice, or Moshe (his Hebrew name), worked with the livestock and spent most days outdoors. He was a shepherd and each morning he took his flock to the valley and low hillsides where there were many streams and lush grasses. The warm breezes, the occasional sounds of a turtle dove and the incessant baas of sheep, created a soothing rhythm to his day.

Moshe was at peace when he was outdoors, whether tending to his sheep or planting seeds in the earth. He found refuge there and was deeply consoled by nature's hum.

His hands told the story of his life. Though normal in size, to me they seemed larger. Cracks and calluses formed on many of his fingers, muscles and tendons expanded, resulting in wider fingers and thicker palms. Many years later, arthritis played havoc with his fingers, twisting and deforming them, rendering them less useful, mirroring how he felt about himself when he retired. With these hands, he carried new-born lambs from the fields and later large bags of grain on the dairy farm.

He was also responsible for shearing and milking the sheep and milking the cows. He loved it. The *refet* (cowshed) was his sanctuary. Moshe was a very nurturing man and found it was less stressful to be with animals, than with human beings. The dairy had a variety of barns and open spaces, as well as stalls for pregnant cows and sheep.

On one occasion, I recall watching him help deliver a calf. The water sac was already severed and fluid was gushing out when the front hooves slowly emerged out of the vulva. Although the hooves seemed to be facing down, suggesting a non-breached position, they remained frozen in state.

Moshe found some thick rope to fasten around the two hooves and began to gently pull the calf out. I was surprised, if not shocked to see how quickly the pinkish snout became visible, followed by the head, body, hind hoofs and tail. My father then took a thin piece of cotton cloth, wrapped it around a tiny twig, and used it to clear the new-born calf's nasal passage of any remaining amniotic fluid and mucous. The calf, with matted hair, stood up almost immediately and vigorously began to suck on one of its mother's teats.

I was mesmerized and numb, witnessing this most natural event and had never seen anything so dramatic at the youthful age of eight. It was the only time in my life that I stood in awe of my father.

Whereas my father flourished in the kibbutz, the same could not be said for my mother. She was prone to sinus- and stress-related headaches, and depending on how hot and humid it was, would sometimes struggle to breath. Her daily work shifted between the cafeteria, the laundry and the library. She washed the dishes and pots, and washed and ironed the clothing.

Although these roles were often rotated, not surprisingly, they were mostly performed by women. She didn't mind working indoors—in fact she preferred it—but it certainly wasn't as stimulating and fulfilling as my father's work.

Besides, my mother had a class consciousness and had "airs" about herself, and felt that this work was beneath her. When she worked in the library it was different, because there she could take time to read a magazine or rifle through shelves of books.

She felt lonely and found it difficult to adapt to kibbutz life. In Holland, she had her own home, her own clothing, and her children nearby. Now everything was shared, clothing, property, and children. Her children no longer identified only with their parents, they identified with an extended family, a whole community. This was difficult to accept, especially for a mother and a woman who survived the war.

Except for Moshe's brother and his wife, there were no other people she felt close to. She longed to be with our extended family in America, and she missed her brother, Leo, who was murdered in Sobibor, and who she had always relied on. She was still in a state of mourning! Haven or not, the transition into kibbutz life was less than idyllic for all of us.

One individual who had a profound impact on me was Beersheba, my Hebrew tutor. A soft-spoken woman, in her late thirties, Beersheba had long black hair, speckled with grey that she wore in a single braid. She always wore a simple white blouse and black pants. Rimless glasses gave her a studious yet approachable demeanor.

I don't know whether I was the only child being tutored at that time, but I certainly felt special. I craved affection and understanding, and because I was deeply bruised, I kept my true self hidden from plain view.

Yet this woman, on what seemed like a daily basis, tutored me in Hebrew, gave me books to read, allowed me to come late to class, and basically nurtured me, in a way my mother could not, or I would not allow. I became an avid reader. The greater command I had over the Hebrew language, the more I read. I was eager to learn, to escape and to block out what I couldn't control.

One book series that totally captivated me was called *Hasamba*, adventure stories about teenagers helping the Haganah, the Jewish paramilitary force, to fight the British in Palestine, prior to Israel's nationhood. These teenagers smuggled information and weapons in their backpacks for the Haganah representatives. Tough, scrappy Israeli boys and girls, not unlike the East Side Kids in American films. I wanted to be like them.

The daily routines for a six-year-old were quite uniform. I didn't mind it being so specific; in fact, it gave me structure and security. I knew what to expect and what was expected of me. I awoke at 6.30, washed, brushed my teeth and dressed. All the young children dressed alike: short khaki pants with shoulder straps that buttoned in front and back and a short-sleeved light-colored shirt.

After dressing I went outside where I joined a bunch of other children, and led by an adult, we ran barefoot cross-country style, through various terrain in and around the kibbutz. Whether it was too costly to buy shoes or, as some thought, healthier to be barefoot, I could not recall ever wearing shoes in the kibbutz.

I enjoyed those vigorous daily runs, and looked forward to the breakfast that followed. After three hours of class time, we took our lunch to the fields. The black bread slathered with mayonnaise, filled with scallion greens was baked by the noon day sun, becoming crunchy as toast and I never grew tired of it.

We spent two hours working in the fields harvesting grapes, eating some and taking little snoozes in the shade of the vines. Sometimes, we set large tarps around olive trees, and milked the branches of green olives, scooped them off the canvas and packed them into wooden crates.

The free time after dinner was devoted to playing on the big lawn near the dining hall. The lights would go out in the dorms about 8 p.m. Although it sounds mundane, to me the daily experience was rich, sweet, predictable and secure, and created a rhythm which was as soothing as it was exhausting. The sky was clear and I slept well.

One evening a week was reserved for outdoor movies. Families gathered on the lawn with beach chairs and blankets, sweets and soft drinks, to watch films projected on a large screen draped on the side of a barn. The films were usually of a patriotic variety, often with a socialist bent, or were vintage 1940s films like Tarzan (with Johnny Weismuller) or Abbott and Costello.

One night after the lights had been shut, I snuck out of the dorm and climbed a concrete wall. There was a full moon and my shadow was long as I walked on top of the wall connecting the two dorms. The wall was meant to divide the rest of the kibbutz from the dorm area, so that the children could feel safe and intimate with their surroundings. It was a foot thick and nine feet tall but I didn't have any trouble navigating my way.

Like a sleepwalker, where was I going, especially at this hour? The mystery, to others, was resolved a few days thereafter. It seems that I quietly strolled into the other dorm and came back a few minutes later with a large stamp album. But, unlike other thieves, who take property for personal gain and profit, I felt compelled to share "my" new stamp album with all the other children.

Naturally, I was caught, reprimanded and forced to return the album to its rightful owner. It was clear that I still felt like the outsider, envious of the popularity of other children, and that I hoped the album would make me accepted by my peers. It did exactly the opposite.

It seemed that every day, in those first six months in Beit HaShita, was fraught with conflict and embarrassment. There were bullies everywhere, and I was the new kid in the neighborhood, the Dutch boy. The more conflict I experienced, the more I withdrew, and the more time I spent in the library with Beersheba. I felt stuck, ambivalent, neither enjoying the kibbutz environment nor feeling a bond with my parents, so it came as no surprise that I rarely visited my parents' cottage.

However, there were exceptions, and on one such occasion my father could tell that I was not happy, and more importantly that I seemed hurt, physically. I had a large welt and a couple of scratches under my left eye, a bruised arm, a bruised right knee, and a slightly swollen lip.

My father was not known as a big talker nor as a mentor; he much preferred the role of simple worker and problem solver. He asked me what had happened, and I, never wanting to show my vulnerable side, said, "I fell into a hole". There was a pause, and he replied, "Well the next time you fall in a hole, make sure to take a stick with you." I took the hint. A week later, I no longer had problems with these boys. In fact, one of them, Alon, became my close friend.

I learned the language quickly. I was fluent in Hebrew in less than a year and Beersheba was no longer central in my life. My childhood that until then, at best, had been uneven, now flourished. I felt as though a major weight had been lifted off my shoulders and that my calloused feet floated above the ground. A burst of energy not experienced before enveloped me, new friendships formed, adolescent adventures abounded—it was an exhilarating time.

A series of adventures followed, one more exciting than the next.

With a gaggle of friends, I explored the many caves nearby. The caves held mysteries; darkness, thick spider webs, odd shaped bones, slimy walls, moss and strange sounds. Scared off by some noises or movement, we rushed down the hills like mountain goats, feet barely touching the ground, zig-zagging past gravely stones, clusters of irises and poppies, tufts of grass, and an assortment of bramble bushes.

At times, we imagined ourselves to be Maccabees. An ancient Hebraic army fighting the evil forces that threatened us. Our mighty wooden swords and homemade bows and arrows overwhelmed our mock enemies in our quixotic play. Each adventure and activity created favorable experiences and memories, and like a montage, produced fluidity and wholesomeness.

Finally, I felt I belonged! I was fully engaged in the fabric of everyday life. My fondest memories of that time were the holidays. I loved Purim, when my sister was dressed as Queen Esther and I was dressed and danced as a Cossack.

Succoth, the harvest festival was my favorite. The Sukkah and the communal feasts that were prepared were unforgettable. Building my first Sukkah, from strong wooden branches, two inches thick, evenly staked into the earth two feet apart was not just a collaborative effort, but symbolically a recognition of my own personal harvest.

The Sukkah was shaped into a rectangular pattern, and we wove young sapling branches horizontally in and out between every other vertical branch, creating secure walls on three sides. Patches of sky showed between the roof branches, and clusters of grapes and thin branches laden with green olives were hung on the interior walls.

On a rough, wooden table, lay baskets of carrots, potatoes, cabbages, leeks, and melons. The cacophony of sounds, the buzzing of bees and flies, the croaking of frogs, and the distant high-pitched howls of jackals, blended with the pungent perfume of fresh ripened fruits and vegetables. All this under a canopy of stars created a bacchanal for the senses that transported me to a place of peace and wonderment.

One day, a group of us were lifted up onto a flatbed truck and driven to the Gilboa mountain range, a short distance away. It was a special trip because the hot, dry, dusty wind (*khamsin*) was pervasive and we could go swimming in a mountain spring. The surface of the flatbed truck was made from metal and we hopped up and down to minimize the burning heat under our feet.

Fortunately, we reached the mountain range fifteen minutes later, quickly jumped off the truck and followed a winding dirt road that took us to the middle of the mountain range.

It was late spring, the heat was oppressive, but the gush of colors was glorious: there were purple and black irises, hearty purple globe thistles, red poppies, white and yellow flowers I did not know, and olive trees.

As we marched forward we passed many streams that nurtured this floral panorama. Somehow King David's curse of making the Gilboa barren, in response to hearing of King Saul and his sons' fate at the hands of the Philistines, was not adhered to by Mother Nature.

We reached our destination after an hour's hike. As we neared, the earth became more a beige-brown and was caked, with grey-white gravely rocks, that hid blue and red flowers. Some trees and tufts of small grasses were still visible. In the distance, we saw the Jezreel Valley and the city of Bet She'an, and we heard the rush of water nearby.

The mountainside was carved out and shaped like an amphitheater, but instead of a stage there was a mountain stream which dissolved into a small body of water. The natural pool was about thirty by forty feet wide, deep and cold. The two guides serving as lifeguards, sat on the rocks nearby and watched us swim in nature's bounty. We stayed for quite a while, eating our lunch and throwing pebbles into the water, but left suddenly when gunshots were heard nearby.

I later learned that Arabs, possibly Jordanians, were shooting in our direction. As a boy of seven or eight I had no sense of the hatred felt by Arabs and Palestinians towards us. I never found out if that was what really happened, but I certainly remembered being frightened. Though our guides were armed, I felt no measure of safety—have I ever felt truly safe? — and instead wanted to run away.

It was late in the afternoon when we left, and the sun busy elsewhere allowed the truck surface to cool. Now it was merely warm and comforting. The guides, eager to shift our attention away from the gunshots and keep everyone calm led us in song. These songs, "Myim, Myim Be Sasson", "Hevanoo Shalom Alechem" and "Hey Da Ro'oma, Hey Da Roma Le Eilat" sung in unison were songs of hope and struggle that filled us with pride and bravado.

The adventures of the day, both pleasant and shocking were sizzling my mind and normally would be ripe for conversation, but my friends and I were so tired, that we barely ate our dinner. In fact, not even the games after dinner occurred, and we promptly went to bed at 7.30.

I was about eight when we got another puppy, whom we named Gura or "puppy" in Hebrew. Gura was a German shepherd mix, the result of a German shepherd female and a male who was half wild dog, half wolf.

As a result, she looked a little darker in coloring as compared to the normal dark brown and blond mantle of a pure-bred German shepherd. However, her snout, eyes, ears, intelligence, and general size mimicked the German shepherd to a tee. She was true to her breed and very protective.

People made a wide berth around my parents' cottage whenever they passed by. I felt safe with her next to me and believed that she understood me better than anyone else. Like Whitey, Gura became another important marker on the road to my development.

The older I became, the less I felt as an outsider and the more I fantasized about joining a Zionist youth corps called the No'ar or Gadna, that helped protect the kibbutz against outside intruders. The Gadna was made up of teen-age boys and girls who were guided and trained so that their induction at age eighteen into the Haganah (the paramilitary force that became the Israel Defense Forces (IDF)) was smoother.

In retrospect, the kibbutz of that time was a place where everyone knew their role, knew where they were going, and knew their limits.

This gave me an immense sense of security. As a ten-year-old, I understood my place in the community, my responsibilities and relationships with my sister, my parents and my friends. It allowed me to experience a delayed childhood. I felt an immense sense of trust, which from my view is the prerequisite for growth and understanding.

Previously, I did not have that foundation, nor the recognition given to me at Beit HaShita, and thus drifted having no core nor sense of belonging. As a result, until the kibbutz, my childhood experience vacillated between loss, anger and mistrust. This was my default mechanism, and even with my new sense of belonging, feelings of rage and longing would surface from time to time, well into my thirties.

Though I fantasized about joining the Gadna, I was having much too much fun just being a child. If I wasn't exploring caves in the mountainside, my friends and I were hanging out in the granary, standing on top of the bags of grain throwing big, black rat-eating snakes at one another, or I could be gathering mushrooms from the moist dark earth in the forest. The land and forces of nature, almost by design, offered us one spectacle after another.

One day it snowed, an event unheard of in Israel, covering everything with a white quilt filled with diamonds. Most of the kids had never seen snow before, and they rushed outside to feel the wet cold on their cheeks and swallowed it wherever they could. It was not long before they realized their bare feet were bluish-red in color and stung like hot coals from the cold.

9

But this bounty of joy was not to last. While my father, sister and I thrived in kibbutz life, my mom couldn't adjust. Four years had passed and she still had the headaches and occasional shortness of breath. She still longed to be closer to her extended family and was less and less happy with the climate and the communal nature of the kibbutz.

There must have been prolonged discussions between our parents and Oom Jules and Tante Emmy, because in early 1953 both families left the kibbutz, with the intent of emigrating to the US. The move itself seemed quite simple because all we carried were our meager belongings: some clothing, photos, jewelry and other small mementos.

Marja and I felt a tremendous loss. Uprooted once again, for me there was a loss of the community and friendships that had become my extended family and a loss of the security that I had finally felt. Those feelings could never mend and trust was ever fleeting. I clutched on to a photo of Gura, as we drove away from the kibbutz towards Ein Sara.

Ein Sara was a village with many raised bungalows that looked like they were built in a hurry and were meant to house people who were in a hurry themselves. Except for the small, white box-like bungalows built on stilts, the earth was barren, and except for the laughter of children, seemed lifeless. The village was in the north and not far away from the tourist-friendly coastal city of Nahariya, and less than an hour to Beirut and Damascus.

We stayed only a few months and I remember Ein Sara through a series of unrelated visual images: a castle nearby, a man nicknamed "abba Gazoz" from whom we bought sodas and ice cream, a small area of tall stately oak and juniper trees, Mr. Friedman's turkeys nervously pecking away near our bungalow, a forest of cacti, and a single paved road that connected Ein Sara to Nahariya.

Ein Sara did not feel real to me. It was a small transient community of people, like a bus stop, all waiting to go somewhere else. I knew by this time that we were going to America, but I could not visualize what that meant. All I felt was a longing to go back to the kibbutz and that even this new alien environment seemed better to me than going to America.

Once again, I felt uprooted, the deck of cards was reshuffled, and a new game was going to be played. It was as though someone pressed the default button, returning me to an earlier mental state of anxiety that I did not want to revisit.

My parents were sweet loving people who knew little about what was best for their children, let alone what was best for themselves. Their scars were so deep, that there was little chance they could see beyond their ancient wounds—how could anyone?

I was no longer accustomed to living at my parents' home. The dorms had created a therapeutic distance from them and a daily regimen that I welcomed as my sanctuary.

To make up for that loss, I decided to build a treehouse. A separate home, from where I could observe others but not be seen. I found an old oak tree, with roots sticking out of the ground, and many low-hanging branches. I climbed up into the thicker foliage so that I could neither be seen from below, nor from a short distance away. From this vantage point I could see the cottages in the distance, a bunch of kids playing and a small black and white dog. This was where I would build my treehouse, my hideaway.

I gathered small branches, maybe an inch thick, and with some twine I fastened them together. Some were perpendicular to one another and others were diagonal.

When I finished, I had created a platform that was about three feet by two feet. I climbed up to my perch and placed my foundation so that it was snugly wedged in between two sturdy branches. For comfort I added a cardboard layer, and for security I strung a cluster of empty cans together under a canopy of leaves.

As a result, I could hear the tin sounds quite a distance away, if my hiding place was ever uncovered. This achievement gave me immense pride.

There were many times, secure in my little hideaway, that I watched the villagers going about their daily routines, or heard my aunt Emmy's booming voice calling me to come home for lunch. On those occasions, I went home totally content, knowing that I had my own secret hidden world, where I was safe, independent, apart and yet near.

I had no routines, except for a half day of school, no friends and no sense of where I was going. The treehouse was my sanctuary, but with ample time I also explored the area around the village. Whereas most of my experience at Ein Sara was a blur, there were several memories that are still quite vivid.

I remember walking into the forest of cacti, the air was hot and dry, and it was difficult to breath. The towering cacti, like green giants, lost some of their spines whenever a slight breeze occurred and these invisible missiles attacked one's clothing and bare skin. Somehow, the sun was less merciful in this forest than elsewhere. The cacti forest served as another sanctuary and I went there quite often.

Nearby there was a large track of land that had many grapefruit trees, and it is there that I met Ahmed, the young man who guarded and tended the citrus plantation. Ahmed lived in a small wooden shack with a tin roof. A bed and a sack of couscous filled the space. The walls were decorated with pages ripped from Life magazine with photos of Hollywood starlets.

These sirens promised everything with their beauty and beckoned him to travel west to lands unknown and possible fulfillment. Outside he kept his horse and tools. It was Ahmed who showed me how to pick prickly pears (*Sabras*) from the cactus and how to ride a horse. I learned to nail an open can to the end of a broom stick, so that the open end faced out, perpendicular to the end of the stick.

All I had to do was look for the deep red-colored pears with fewer spines, place the open can over the ripe fruit, twist, and catch it in the can. Then I emptied the fruit into a pail half filled with cold water. I sliced both ends and made a vertical incision in the skin, peeling it off.

The cactus pear or sabra with its tough skin and sweet interior, personified the native-born Israeli, who were informally called Sabras. The fruit tasted sweet and foreign, the picking process was long and, invariably, I was itchy for days. Comparatively speaking, I think if Eve received a prickly pear instead of an apple, human evolution might still be in its infancy.

My father and uncle found temporary work in Nahariya, while my mom and aunt tried to make their respective homes as normal as they could, which included sending us to school. Both families left for America a few months later, and no matter how hard they tried to maintain a sense of normalcy, the anticipation of taking a ship to America created excitement in the family.

For me it reawakened my anxiety. I felt I was drifting aimlessly, as in a dream, the tides pulled me one way and then another, I felt the warm breezes against my face and the flutter of birds nearby, but I could not see nor grasp them.

It was not long after I met Ahmed that I was counseled by the local police about him. Essentially, I was told that Ahmed could not be trusted and that I should not associate with him. I was surprised and confused.

Years later, when I became politically active and read about the development of Israel, I thought about this incident. It somehow fit into a historical pattern where cultures clashed, land was not to be shared and trust was not to be found. This division between "us" and "them", between victors and losers, where people were mistrusted and marginalized, not only clashed with my sense of fairness, but reminded me all too well of another time, when society needed to be "cleansed" and children like me were expunged.

A few days after the police visit, Uncle Jules came to our bungalow with a small black and white fox terrier puppy that he had found under his bungalow. There were three, and he kept one for himself, and gave one to a neighbor, and one to us. It took forever before we bonded. She was already four months old, independent, and looked like she was old enough to fend for herself, while I was still hurting from my previous loss, and anxious that we would soon leave again.

It seemed that dogs and children grew up very quickly in these parts. But I fell for her, I couldn't help myself, and she, like Whitey and Gura, smoothed all the parched emotions that I felt. My parents named her Gura again, and like her predecessors, she followed me around. If Marja and I played on the deck at the castle, Gura insisted on coming. If we went to Abba Gazoz to get ice cream, Gura followed along.

This was both a blessing and a curse, because two months later she was the cause of an accident. On that morning, my sister and I were on our way to the paved road to wait for the school bus that would take us to Nahariyya, and Gura followed us. I yelled at her to go home, but she wouldn't listen. As we neared the road, I could see the school bus coming and Gura standing in the middle of the road. I yelled at her once more and then as I rushed to shoo her away from the oncoming bus, I was hit by a sand truck that was slowing down, and coming from the other direction.

I blacked out and when I awakened found myself lying down in the back of the school bus. I was on my way to the hospital in Nahariya and spent the next six days there, with a concussion, dizzy, nauseous, bewildered and depressed. Fear of dying, which until then lay mostly dormant, now haunted me, and the accident was a rude reminder that life is precious and that we are only a few degrees removed from possible extinction.

Two months later, the Gosler families received cash for the crossing and word that Tante Rose would sponsor them in the United States. We packed our few suitcases and boarded the bus that would take us to Haifa. I sat in the back and I saw that Gura was following us, my eyes welled up as she became smaller and smaller and morphed into a lump in my throat.

I could not swallow.

PART 3

AMERICA 1953 - 1960

10

I think I first sensed my recurring anxiety as a persistent tightness in my chest when I was about eleven. I am sure that these subterranean waves happened well before we left Israel, if not earlier in Holland, but I didn't recall being aware of them until this point.

Leaving Eretz Israel ripped my head open to the universe. This land represented physical beauty, safety, joy, strength, clarity, independence and community, and I felt utterly diminished as we boarded the ship that took us to Naples (Italy), a week later.

As the ship moored in the bay of Naples, many little boats came from every direction with trinkets to sell: shiny jewelry, cheap watches, scarves, beads, oranges, cheese and cameras. They were like piranhas ready to overwhelm even the youngest tourist who got in their path.

Squinting and nearly blinded from the glaring sun, I followed my parents along the rising, narrow streets to our *pensione*. A long, sticky section of flypaper filled with dead black flies greeted us as we entered our lodgings. A square room with a high ceiling, big windows flooded with sunlight and brass beds was our temporary quarters.

Outside the windows, I could see laundry flapping in the sea breezes and below in the alleyways I saw fat-bellied rats and even larger cats, each ignoring the other, but like opposing street gangs, patrolling their own turf. Compared to Eretz Israel, land of milk and honey, Naples was poor, transient and foreign. The stop in Naples was simply to change ships, from a Mediterranean passenger ship to an ocean liner, and we only stayed for three days.

The SS Constitution was considered a fast-modern ship, simply decorated and more informal than its European counterparts. A few years after our voyage it became famous because a few "I Love Lucy" television shows were filmed on it, in addition to some well-regarded films.

For me, the voyage couldn't end quickly enough! Whether it was related to my recent concussion, fear of the unknown, or the waves of the sea, I heaved my guts out over the lower deck each day.

In contrast, Marja and cousins, Marion and Johnny (Marion's brother who was born in Israel), ran around and enjoyed the freedom of movement, the sunlight and the sea. I felt like I was entering a dark tunnel, with no respite and no psychological treehouse in sight.

The dining-room served as a multi-purpose space for food and entertainment. Although the food was tasty and elegantly presented, I could neither savor nor digest it as everyone else did. Instead, I was consumed by my physical misery and emotional anxiety.

Next to me in the dining room sat a man in his late twenties, narrow and tall, with dark hair, bronze-colored skin, and Asian features. He held a soup spoon in mid-air and the gesture distracted me from my suffering.

I noticed he had a long nail on his pinky finger that contrasted to his nine other fingernails that were conventionally short. I wondered if he had some sort of abnormal nail growth, where some grew faster than the others, and I was equally concerned that the one and half inch nail might be used as a weapon.

Occasionally, my stomach did not rebel and allowed me to remain in the dining room, where after-dinner games like Bingo were played and movies were shown. I saw films before in the kibbutz, but they were either propaganda films or of the Tarzan and Abbot and Costello variety.

I was entranced by the film, "One Touch of Venus" with Ava Gardner and Robert Walker. Not only did the film quiet my stomach, but to see Ava Gardner behind sheer curtains on a moonlit night left me wanting to leave everything behind, and dissolve into the celluloid.

11

The SS Constitution entered the NYC harbor on November 30th, 1953. Both Gosler families were on deck, along with a multitude of others to see the Statue of Liberty. A collective cheer that became louder as we neared the crowned lady was followed by the clicking of cameras and a deep sigh of relief as we drifted slowly towards a throng of people waiting at Pier 84.

In contrast, a dark cloud seemed to hover over me, no matter where I went. The generalized anxiety and the aftershocks of the concussion continued to plague me. I was nauseous whenever I travelled by bus or car and whenever the weather turned cloudy or misty, I had migraines and strained to see more clearly.

Our family stayed in Brooklyn, near Avenue U, with Tante Judith and her husband, Oom Caballes. Tante Betje, my great-aunt also lived there, and I shared a bedroom with her. Tante Betje, a short, sturdy woman with pristine white hair, sharp wit and warm smile, became my confidante.

I appreciated her warmth and attentiveness and felt special when I was in her company. At eighty-three, walking with a cane, and living in her daughter's home, she was mentally sharp and high spirited, but worried about being marginalized by her own family. I do not remember much of our five-month stay, but I had a sense that both our host and my parents were glad that we left when we did. If not for shoveling the snow off the many stoops on our block, I might have considered our stay a mirage.

In late spring we moved, along with uncle Jules' family, to Rockaway Park to a house where other relatives had stayed five years earlier. The red brick two-story house was close to the beach and boardwalk.

Both Gosler families lived in the basement and we entered the house through a concrete paved rear yard, next to the enclosed outdoor showers. An interior door separated our family dwelling from my uncle's.

My parents were eager to find work and my mother began cleaning nearby homes, while my father got a job in the garment industry through the efforts of Tante Rose.

During that summer, I combed the beach for empty bottles, two cents for a small bottle and five cents for a large one. In my pursuit of pocket change, I was keenly aware of life on the beach, but remained a voyeuristic outsider. I watched the people sitting on blankets dabbing themselves with suntan lotion or baby oil, teenagers roughhousing or making out with their girlfriends, eating and going swimming.

My observations made me acutely aware how detached I was, not just as a foreigner, but how empty I felt inside. I wanted to recapture the freedom and camaraderie of the kibbutz, belonging to a community and working on shared goals. I wanted to go back to Israel.

The summer also meant that 116th Street, the main commercial street in Rockaway Park, transformed from a quiet sandy street into a bustling, tourist attraction. White-painted stalls were built near the boardwalk to sell soda, cotton candy, sweet peanuts and freshly made pizza. The pungent food smells, Bill Haley and the Comets blaring in the background, the people traffic and the salty sea air, combined to create a fantasy oasis.

For me, the pizza stall was a marvel to watch. The men with their wife beater T-shirts and heads covered with knotted white kerchiefs, would twirl and stretch the flattened dough, throw it in the air and it landed on floured forearms to be stretched again and then set on long handled floured pizza boards. After the pie was shoveled into the wood fired ovens, the aroma became a narcotic and the exotic taste was heavenly. I couldn't get enough of it.

The summer was also a time when I played "Cowboys and Indians" with the neighborhood boys, and like a true outsider, always wanted to be an Indian. Watching the Lone Ranger and Hopalong Cassidy, I understood very quickly that the native Americans were marginalized in America and were characterized either as savages or men without intelligence or ambition. I identified with them immediately.

On Sunday evenings, we watched the "Betty White Show" on an almost round-shaped TV screen at a neighbor's home. Televisions were still a new phenomenon and were major pieces of furniture and a luxury that our family could not afford.

Living near the coast was a pleasant experience until the storms arrived. Late in the summer of 1954, there were two hurricanes, Carol and Edna, that hit Long Island and the north-east coast. The basement flooded from the rains and everyone pitched in with buckets and mops to rescue the furniture and floors of our home.

On such occasions it seemed, as though the ocean and the bay waters met at our basement. My father, ever the good Samaritan, went out after the storms subsided to see what damage there was to our flat as well as to other homes on the block. There were scattered branches, leaves, garbage and puddles everywhere, but this time there was also an electric cable down.

My father was about to move the cable to the side of the street when Marja, sensing danger, yelled "Poppy don't pick it up!" This was the second time that Marja, aged nine, saved poppy from harm.

The first time was in Israel the year before when my father was about to put on his boots and Marja noticed a yellow scorpion inside one of them. Her scream made the scorpion scamper away, but not before poppy smashed it with the other boot. Marja and I were vigilant in protecting our parents from harm.

There were so many incidents where an untimely or wrong decision meant the difference between life and death. It is likely that if my parents didn't leave in the middle of the night, that just like my maternal grandmother, they too would have been captured, or if -while sitting in that barber's chair my two-year old voice was heard by the passing Nazi soldiers, I too would not be here today. I was constantly aware that life can be snuffed out or diminished in a nanosecond, and that I must strive to overcome all obstacles to preserve it.

The end of summer also meant that, for the first time, I would attend an American school. The basic English language comprehension I had learned in Israel had improved sufficiently for me to communicate with the world around me and made it easier to form friendships.

As I was stretching outward I was also being pulled from within—pubescence. On the surface all seemed fine, but my nights were different. Many nights I had the same recurring nightmare: the Nazi SS were trying to catch me and I couldn't get away. As the Nazis neared, I woke up startled, full of angst, and—for some reason—I was always caught naked.

These nights were also my first memories of masturbation, and the raw pleasure and its sweet exhaustion, would lull me back to sleep.

Whether it related to my disturbing dream, or the pubescent pipe dreams of a pre-teen, I had all sorts of seductive fantasies about girls. It was all so arousing; watching them, making eye contact, possibly touching them, but I had no clue or confidence as to how to achieve any of that.

In retrospect, I wish my father had taken me aside to share his feelings and thoughts about his own youth and desires, I definitely needed guidance.

Sometimes, on the beach I watched the girls and women walk by, and found myself awkwardly aroused. I watched them lay down on blankets: long legs, little pubic curls on inner thighs, nipples and swimsuit straps, lipstick and suntan lotion. It was a blur of sensuality.

At other times, I sat under the boardwalk and watched women in bellowing skirts through the cracks between the boards, hoping to see whatever I was lucky enough to see. No doubt my sexual fantasies, hair growing in all sorts of places, and a deeper voice all conspired to produce dreams of being caught in embarrassing situations. The nightmares occurred less frequently as I became more comfortable with my own adolescence.

Adolescence in the Jewish tradition also meant that soon the transition from boy to adulthood was to be celebrated through the religious initiation ceremony of the Bar Mitzvah.

Tante Rose, who emigrated to the US in the late 20s, was the matriarch of the Gosler clan in America. She and her husband developed a line of maternity clothing, and their small company thrived. Because she blazed the path for others to follow, it was natural that she became the "host" who supported the newly emigrated members of the Gosler families, as she had done for my uncles and aunts, the Trompetters, five years earlier.

She also helped us. I was twelve years old and my parents hoped that Tante Rose would support the Bar Mitzvah lessons and celebration party. This was a major expense for our family but Tante Rose considered it, and obliged.

I had no idea why this rite of passage was considered so profound since my parents neither attended synagogue, nor celebrated holidays, nor talked to me about its importance in Jewish practice.

In fact, until that point in time I hadn't identified as a Jew or for that matter as a person with any religious preference. I agreed to meet with a rabbi after school to study the Torah and the rituals necessary for the Bar Mitzvah because I had been promised a suit.

I never had a suit and I considered it an important status symbol. Since I still spoke Hebrew fluently, I grasped the meaning of the Torah lessons and remembered the prayers easily. I spent much more time correcting the rabbi's Hebrew enunciations than on the lessons to be learned.

The rabbi was spared the agony of continuing the Bar Mitzvah lessons, because Tante Rose withdrew her support, after an argument with my mother. As a result, I did not have a Bar Mitzvah. I was upset, not because I had to find an alternative passage to manhood, but because I didn't get the suit.

A few weeks after the sudden end to my Bar Mitzvah, an incident crystalized why I was not simply an outsider but an outsider who was a Jew. While walking with two strong hulking twins each wearing a colorful yarmulke, we were accosted by a group of kids who called us dirty Jews and said, "Why don't you leave our neighborhood."

The twin boys, Barry and Levy, wrestled them to the ground before I even got involved, and the confrontation ended a few minutes later.

At that moment, I neither felt victorious or particularly proud of being a Jew. If anything, I felt confused. This was the first time—outside of my Bar Mitzvah studies—that I was identified as being a Jew, and synonymous with slime. In Israel I wasn't a Jew, I was a Zionist, in Holland I wasn't a Jew, I was a Dutch boy. In our family, we did not pray, attend temple, or observe any religious rituals. Why would I identify with being Jewish? How ironic!

My first three years of life were all to do with being Jewish and yet the distinct awareness of being Jewish didn't resonate in me until I was twelve. If anything, given my experience and my parents suffering, I am not surprised that until that time, I psychologically blocked it out.

There may have been other instances of antisemitism that I experienced, but they must have been very subtle in form since I don't recall any. Over my life, I have been preoccupied with tracing my family roots and by extension, the history of the Jewish people.

I have read about the causes of antisemitism, be they religious, economic, cultural, or in political form, but I can never understand why Israel and many Jews wrap themselves so tightly in righteous indignation when it comes to the Holocaust. As I said before, I neither want to forgive or forget, but to put the Holocaust on what seems like a religious pedestal, is to invite guilt and further anti-Semitic sentiments.

The incident also made me realize that America unlike the kibbutz, was about separateness, of "I" and "Thou", where some people belonged and others didn't. I began to see my Jewishness through a lens heavily influenced by my family's wartime experience and as an immigrant.

In America, for many years thereafter, I was in a self-imposed ghetto. Even at that time, when I would see a gathering of people, dressed up for the High holidays, standing in front of a Synagogue, I would make a wide turn to avoid them. For some reason the gathering seemed artificial to me since I knew that most of the gathered did not attend the synagogue on a weekly basis.

I also wonder if there was some resentment that I was harboring that I did not understand at that time. I grew up not trusting organized religion nor any large entity that in theory advocated for me. I always believed that they were not advocating for me, but only for the chosen few: the wealthy and the well-connected, which usually meant the same people. Besides, why do I need a guide or intermediary to find God? Instead, I leaned toward individualism, collaboration and the importance of family through which I gained my spiritualism.

My resentment is not just against the politics and what I perceived as the superficiality of the synagogue, but is also reserved for God. I have always wondered that if there's a God how can he / she / it have stood aside during WWII. How could God have allowed the massacre of so many people, of little children. Why?!

My incident and the chasm that developed between Tante Rose and my parents added to a restlessness that they felt. My father hoped to find work as a butcher, but found that European and American butchering differed greatly. Moreover, his English was poor and unions were rife with nepotism, making it even more difficult. He found part-time work, but neither liked it nor did it pay a living wage. Later, when he worked full time in the garment industry, he was equally disappointed by the nature of his work.

On the other hand, my mom was more content than she had been in many years, but continued to suffer from chronic sinus headaches and elevated blood pressure. I cannot remember a time prior to my mother finding work, that she was truly happy. Marja was attending elementary school, as was cousin Marion. I sensed that my parents were at a crossroad, though happy to be in America, they were neither comfortable nor content and argued a lot.

The winter passed quickly and I looked forward to warmer weather and the playfulness of summer. I was nearly thirteen, listened to my parents half-heartedly, became more aware of my parents' financial limitations and longed to have the material things that my friends had. I wanted to impress them, to feel like an equal, and to accomplish this I was willing to tempt fate. I still collected bottles off the beach and often walked from Rockaway Park to the nude beach at Reese Park and back.

On occasion, I found a quarter or some other small treasure, like a wedding band, but mostly it was unrewarding, and the routine began to feel more like a chore.

One day I saw a kid, about my age, discretely eyeing a teenage couple on a blanket. They were oblivious to the world around them, listening to music on their radio, and were ripe for prey. Suddenly they got up and dashed towards the ocean, one after the other, splashing the water as they dove under a wave. I heard their distant laughter, as I watched the kid swoop down, pick up a wallet, hide it in his trunks and run away.

I followed him at a safe distance and saw him enter an alleyway, empty the wallet, take out the paper money and drop the wallet on the ground. After he left, I examined the empty wallet and noticed the many coins on the ground. I picked up the coins, counting their worth and realized that the sum was more than what I earned in a full day of bottle collecting.

The 1950s surged on. A strong post-war economic wave, with traditional values still intact, a time when people knew their roles and places in society, an age of innocence.

As a result, without much thought, people left their valuables on their blankets when they went for a swim. I bumped into the same kid a few days later, except that this time he approached me, and we became pals. This was also the beginning of a nefarious new form of employment for me because we worked out a scheme of how to steal valuables off the blankets. We would zero in on a blanket with many valuables and no children. We realized that parents with young children generally divided their time between blanket and water and rarely left the blanket unattended. Somehow young couples were easy, since they spent most of their time focused on one another and were oblivious to the staged mock fights near their blankets. When they went for a swim, one of us would swoop down and put the valuable(s) into our bathing trunks. We would then stage a mock playful fight and run after one another.

We met in the same designated alley and split the "take". Generally, there was five dollars, but one time there was fifty. There were other objects as well, like watches, rings, sun glasses, and once a transistor radio. I realized that instead of earning five to ten dollars per week, I was now reaping twenty or more. I understood that bringing home more than my daily bottle sum would raise my parents' suspicions, so I found an empty lot and buried the excess in a black sock about a foot beneath the earth.

I fantasized about buying a Raleigh English three-speed racer and also wanted to have some easy cash in my pocket. By mid-July, I amassed a large sum of money, enough for the bike plus walking-around money. But, because my parents believed that I was earning money through the daily grind of collecting bottles, I did not think it was wise to purchase the bike until the end of summer.

I stopped this game of "steal and run" after my new-found friend divided the spoils unevenly, giving me a Mickey Mouse watch, while he kept a wad of dollar bills for himself. Throughout my life there would be a duality between the world of hustle, money and self-aggrandizement and the world of collaboration towards the common good. I never told my parents of my nefarious enterprise because, next to lying, stealing was the greatest sin in our family.

12

In late August, our family moved to a chicken farm in Monticello, NY. The move itself was easy, since we took only our clothing, memorabilia, and some bedsheets, linens and towels. Poppy was eager to get away from the garment industry work and looked forward to moving to the chicken farm, where he was hired as the foreman. For me it was yet another emotional upheaval where I had to once again leave the familiar, all that had become home, my friends and my neighborhood and move to places unknown.

The owners of the farm were Russian Jews who owned over one hundred and fifty acres of land and one hundred and fifty thousand chickens. Although the farm was a hundred and fifty acres of mostly open fields, the coops and other buildings including several trailers were concentrated on approximately three acres, near the living quarters.

The main house was large enough to house us, the grandparents, as well as the two households of the joint owners. Bob, his wife Natalie and their children, Richie, Denise and Leslie, occupied one side of the ground floor. Martin, his wife Florence (Bob's sister) and their daughter, Stephanie, lived on the other side of the ground floor. In the back, there was an attached apartment where the grandparents lived. Although the house was bustling with people, it felt cozy.

At first, we lived on the first floor as well, squeezed in between the two families. I am sure that my mother hated the experience and must have thought she was back in the kibbutz, where she had little she could call her own, including a lack of privacy.

Both the grandparents died within two years after we arrived and we were given their apartment. The apartment was modest, we had a separate entrance, privacy and a place we could call home.

A white mixed-breed huskie named Whitey and an assortment of cats who lived outside, completed the small community. Each morning, Florence scrambled a huge amount of eggs and fed the cats on newspaper, or cardboard.

There were cats everywhere, domestic and semi-feral, they interacted with the humans and yet seemed to live in a world of their own. I fondly remember Marja placing her "lilly", her security blanket, in a discreet location under the house upon which one of the cats gave birth.

The trailers housed workers and day-laborers. These people were rarely integrated into the social hub of the farm. They were usually poor white or black men who lived by themselves and were paid in the form of cash and / or groceries. There was a sense of transience about their lives and they remained on the periphery, like semi-domesticated dogs, never to be understood or trusted.

Little did I realize that their experience mirrored my own marginalization. I never felt a sense of belonging. My life was as transient as theirs, but acknowledging the similarities was too painful and I desperately identified with the owners of the chicken farm.

A country road divided the main house and trailers from the coops, tractors, trucks, barns and candling station. On days when it rained or the humidity was high, the sharp acid stench of chicken manure was especially strong, irritating my throat, nostrils, and eyes.

The chicken coops were like cities, crowded with white feathered birds. Yellow chicks were penned in under incubators as though they were in a daycare center. There were long narrow troughs carrying feed to the masses, water spigots to refresh, and nests—one floor above the other—like small apartments with small windows and plenty of electric light. At night, the chickens lay in their nests, the lights eventually went out and the clucking and flapping of wings ceased.

As with crop rotation, the farmers planned when to purchase new chicks and when to remove aging unproductive hens. The latter process usually occurred when the hens turned two or three years old and entered a molting stage.

It was on those occasions that all hands got involved, including Richie and myself. During this ritual, the task was to take one or two hens by their claws (in each hand) and force them into slotted wooden crates. The hens out of fright and desperation flapped their wings and I felt as though they could propel me off the ground into the ceiling of the coop. Once in their crates and stacked on the flatbed trucks, they would settle down. Richie and I didn't know where they were going, but like the Jews in cattle cars during the war, we had no doubt that they would not return.

I entered Monticello Central High as a seventh grader. Once again, I was the outsider in a tight-knit community that had unwritten rules about Blacks, Hispanics, the poor, "hicks" (country people), and foreigners.

On the surface, people got along: Jews and gentiles got along, and Blacks knew their place in the unwritten pecking order although they were already the better athletes on several sports teams.

Hispanics worked in nearby hotels, poor people and "hicks" were tolerated, and foreigners were treated as aliens, although there was always a forced curiosity. Half of the town seemed to be Jewish and the other half Christian. Most of the Jews were shopkeepers, bankers, lawyers, teachers, and hotel owners. The Christians owned farms, gas stations and repair shops, or worked for Sullivan County in one capacity or another. All others noted were mostly invisible and excluded from society. I identified with the latter, as I did when playing Cowboys and Indians.

Although my English was improving, I still felt awkward and at times was bothered by headaches and nausea, a lingering after effect of my concussion. This interfered with my ability to concentrate in school and in my first year I failed some classes. Fortunately, most of the teachers I had were patient and accessible, and by the second year, with improved English, I was able to pass the subjects I had previously failed.

By this time, Richie, who was a year younger than me, became my first close friend in America. He was a fun loving, good student who felt more comfortable in a lab than on a playing field. On the other hand, I, with no parental guidance in my education, just barely passed my courses, but flourished in team sports. In fact, we complimented one another and, whereas Richie helped me with my studies, I would "always have his back".

One day, when we were going to school on the small Monticello school bus, I helped Richie confront a bully. We had just been dropped off in front of the school when this beefy kid started pushing Richie around. Although Richie was fearless, he was no match for this kid, and I jumped in and wrestled the bully to the ground. It was over in a few minutes. Richie and I were surprised, in part, by my coming to his aid and by how easily it was resolved. Neither Richie nor I talked about it afterwards, but I felt not only proud to help him, but also somewhat tickled by my own strength.

Richie and I were inseparable. We played baseball and other sports together and he introduced me to BB guns. Our BB gun target practice sharpened the skills we needed to hunt and kill the field rats that invaded the chicken coops. The field rats were brown, slow moving, scarred creatures, with long tails and bloated stomachs, who dragged themselves over the chicken dung, looking for a cracked egg or a sickly chick. Richie with his trusty 22 and I with a baseball bat entered the coop, like soldiers, decimating the few rodents we saw.

My father was the foreman of the farm and took his job with the same sincerity and dedication that he displayed with everyone and everything. He collected the eggs, some of which he found nestled in the chicken droppings, and put them in round metal mesh baskets. Each basket, filled with eggs weighed about thirty pounds and he lugged them, one in each hand, to another building where they were cleaned and candled.

My mother and Florence cleaned and candled the eggs to make sure they were fresh and unfertilized. It was in this hum of daily life that Marja, now aged eleven, went to the same school that I attended, and slowly developed her own set of friends.

Somehow, though younger than me, she was less restricted by my parents than I was. I was not allowed to stay overnight at other people's homes. My mother always waited for me to come home, even when I turned seventeen. On the other hand, Marja, as a young teen slept over at her friend's homes, many times.

Giving me away as an infant and then returning at age three, angry and disoriented, made my mother even more determined and protective. I think she knew that I had not forgiven her for sending me away and taking me from the Dijkstra's. What we had, at best, was a detente. Her protectiveness only stopped when I moved out of the house.

Slowly, through the passage of time and excellence on the athletic fields, I gained more confidence and some sense of self-esteem. Concurrently, I—chameleon like—copied other people as I tried out different accents, walking strides, hair and clothing styles. I suspect that this was no different from what other teens did, but it meant more to me as an immigrant and outsider. I took it to an extreme.

To be super cool, I walked with a slight bounce, the way cocky young black men walked. I also used Vitalis hair tonic and designed a hanging curl in front on my forehead, that froze during cold weather, becoming a veritable weapon if I jerked my head sideways.

At the same time, I became acutely aware that my ears stuck out and my mother would sometimes rub it in when she would say, "Wat een flaporen heb je!" (What floppy ears you have!) I fumed and smoldered inside but never allowed it to surface, that would have suggested that my ears or her remarks bothered me.

Instead, in the bathroom mirror I pictured how my ears would look flat against my head and pinned them against my head with my hands to see the difference. The world of a teenager is one of prohibition; everything they are or do gets communicated clandestinely, if at all. My search for self-identity meant that I added different features to myself, so that I felt complete.

However, I was more like a caricature wearing many band-aid like stickers that spelled "cool", "tough", "dude", the way some people put travel stickers on their cars to impress others. Even as a youngster I went to extremes to impress my friend Dimo who dared me to pick up a thick section of rope, partially visible on a frozen pond. I needed to impress my friend and not back down. I picked up the rope and promptly fell through the ice. If it wasn't for a young couple who heard Dimo's screams, I would have drowned.

Sports were my foundation for achieving a measure of self-esteem. I excelled in baseball, soccer, track, and basketball. Although I loved basketball the most, my size, rigidity and slowness meant that I only played pickup games or was on an intramural team.

In fact, I loved basketball so much that I played by myself on the farm during the coldest weather, often simply in a T-shirt. My obsession with basketball was so intense, that routinely during gym class I continued shooting hoops while everyone else was already standing on the sidelines waiting for attendance to be taken. This was so frustrating for the physical education teacher that he gave me a used basketball to keep if I agreed to partake in the attendance taking ritual.

There was a very thin line between feeling exalted or desolate. Whether related to the beginning of my teens, my war experience, or being the new kid in town, more often than not, I was in a state of desolation. Lonely and empty, I wandered along Broadway, looking at my reflection in storefront windows, to validate my existence.

One day, while meandering through town, I met a man who started talking to me, and at some point asked me what music I liked. Out of the blue, I mentioned jazz. The man said that he had some good Jazz albums at his place and convinced me to come with him. I was both intrigued, numb and emotionally cut-off, and like a zombie, went with him. We reached a small motel at the west end of Broadway and entered his room.

The next thing I remembered was that my jeans were pulled down along with my underwear, and the guy was going down on me. A volcanic burst of sweetness followed as I came, followed by the guy wiping the scum away with a warm, moist hand towel. It was only then that I noticed another man, with a tattoo on his arm, in a second bed nearby, sleeping.

I left the motel room in a daze. I didn't know what to make of this experience. Should I feel guilty, exhilarated or triumphant? I was totally disoriented. This was yet another time when my consciousness flew outside of my body and hovered above over my hollow self. I quickly started hitchhiking and was lucky to catch a ride right away.

The following day, be it out of curiosity or coincidence, I bumped into the same guy coming out of a bar. It was only then that I realized how tall and rail thin the man was, and that he was black. Again, I felt that familiar paralysis when the guy offered me some change and told me to keep my mouth shut about what happened the day before.

It was at this point that I felt more guilt and self-anger than before, as well as self-doubt about my sexuality. Self-torture and mind games followed:Am I gay, and why did I follow this man?

I did not realize at the time how I appreciated the attention of an older man in contrast to my father's lack of involvement in my life. The confusion about my sexuality as exemplified by the "incident" haunted me for many years.

In fact, the first few sexual experiences I had with women, were as much a validation to me of my heterosexuality as anything else. It was not until the late 1960s, when I formed my political and psychological views, that I felt more confidence and clarity about my sexual orientation.

As I became more proficient in English, my grades improved and I became better acquainted with other students. I met Marc, a kid who also lived on Holmes Road, and we became pals. Although I envied Marc because he was popular, had cars, and was brash, I never allowed him to enter my inner sanctum like Richie. That said, hanging out with Marc meant that I was now in a different social click, and I started to mimic Marc's personality. My demeanor changed. I now displayed a forced cockiness and sarcasm.

In 9th grade I chose Spanish as my foreign language and had a teacher named Mr. Goldberg. He seemed like a caricature of an egghead: with dark unruly hair, thick rimless glasses, a serious stare, and hair desperately escaping from his nose. He wore his pants almost to his chest level, held there by his belt and partially covered by a wide flowery tie.

Mr. Goldberg thought he was encouraging me when he continually stated that I should find Spanish easy to learn because I was proficient in Dutch and Hebrew. Instead of encouragement, I felt embarrassed and irritated whenever he verbally cornered me in that way.

One day, after he singled me out once again, I, without hesitation replied, "Mr. Goldberg, during WWII six million Jews died. What happened to you?!" I said it so quickly, that I couldn't remember what I had said, and it was only days later when bumping into a classmate that I was reminded of what I blurted out. I wasn't scolded or penalized by Mr. Goldberg. In fact, from that point forward he basically ignored me.

I was much more interested in sneaking into the Concord Resort Hotel with Marc. The Concord was regarded as one of the premier Catskill watering holes for affluent Jews who summered there with their families.

Milton Berle, Lucille Ball, Allen & Rossi, Buddy Hackett and Frankie Machito were regular guests and performers at the hotel. An aged Buster Crabbe performed as part of the staff at the indoor pool and would parody how Marilyn Monroe swam. The world's most famous diver, Raul Garcia, who did a Timex commercial with John Cameron Swayze, served as a diving instructor and part-time security guard.

Marc had mentioned that getting into the hotel was a good way of meeting girls, and we snuck in through a hole in the fence near the tennis courts. I don't know what happened to Marc, but I was promptly caught by security and brought to the indoor pool. It was early evening when most people were at dinner and the pool was closed. The security guards started grilling me. Suddenly, Raul Garcia took matters into his own hands, literally, and punched me squarely on the chin, stunning me, and then escorted me off the hotel grounds.

Machito's band performing, "All the World was Going Cha Cha", and the glittering chandeliers, the plush, red carpeting, wafts of cigarette smoke and the alcohol in crystal glasses, was the adult world of forbidden pleasures that lured me back.

A few weeks later, we returned to the hotel without any problems, and had a great time. It was rumored that the security was told to ignore us because hitting a minor was a serious offense that made the hotel libel in any suit filed against it.

It may have been a coincidence or maybe it was calculated, but at exactly the time when I was spreading my social wings, when I was enjoying the Concord social scene and becoming recognized for my soccer and baseball skills, my parents demanded that it was time for me to find a weekend and an after-school job.

My burgeoning social life spiraled downward, as I no longer had time to play sports after school and my weekend social binges at the Concord narrowed. Just at a point when I was becoming more independent and forming a clearer sense of self, my parents—out of some medieval tithe tradition—spite or actual financial need, decided that it was important for me to work part time. My wings clipped, I worked as a helper at Strauss and Sons, a sports houseware store. I don't believe they ever understood how much I was hurt from that experience. And, when I reflect upon that time, how much I resented them still.

This work was followed by summer work at Schneider's Bungalow Colony, where I worked as a soda jerk, made black & white sodas and egg creams and performed various menial tasks that allowed Marja to attend the Schneider day camp for free.

What little control I had over my life and direction was again put on hold, as I reluctantly complied with my parents' wishes. I am sure I didn't earn much money, nor do I recall being allowed to keep any for myself.

This experience of sacrifice solidified my sense of responsibility and commitment to my parents, but at a severe price. The more I helped my parents out, the more it embittered me, and the more enslaved I felt. Hence forward, a job was always synonymous with imprisonment, bitterness, suffocation and a lack of joy.

The Concord was where I wanted to be and realizing I could earn more money there, I decided to apply for a position. I first worked at the ski lodge, where I saw Sugar Ray Robinson's wife and kids tobogganing. My job was hard to describe; one day I was serving hot cocoa, the next day I was handing out boots, skis and poles, and on the third day—most ludicrously—I was showing skiers how to fall properly, as part of a skier's orientation. The latter assignment was most amusing because until then I had never put on skis in my life, nor did I ever do downhill skiing thereafter.

The hotel was run like a mom and pop store, and you were at the whim of the boss, be that Arthur Winarick or his son in law, or your immediate supervisor. Whatever they wanted you to do, you did, or you lost your job.

I was willing to try anything and often convinced my supervisor that I was an expert at doing just about everything. For lunch, I ate in the employee dining hall, where I was surprised to find Leslie Uggams, a newly discovered black "Pop" singer, and her mom eating. Although Ms. Uggams, as a teenager, was performing at the Concord, she was no celebrity, like Sammie Davis Jr., and had to eat with the workers

Soon I found another job within the Concord as an elevator boy in the main building, and that led to being a page boy. A page boy's work was all encompassing. At its core, I tracked down individuals who had phone calls, and if not found, wrote messages that I left in the guest's mailbox.

At times, I bell-hopped, brought soda and ice to guests as part of room service, adjusted lounge chairs and umbrellas at the poolside, and even pimped. I knew a couple of addresses on Liberty Street in Monticello, where guests could fulfil their sexual fantasies. Basically, people who work in hotels learn how to hustle and often take short cuts. Timing was everything.

At hotels like the Concord, the more cash an individual was capable of flashing, the more respect and attention he was given. There were a few professional gamblers who summered at the Concord and they owned and bet on horses, racing dogs and managed boxers. They sat at a table in the sun, smoking cigars, playing cards and scribbling notes on small pieces of paper.

I always imagined that the slips of paper were a discrete way of noting the transference of turf (an urban area each for drug or prostitution traffic) from the loser to the winner of the game. Some of the gamblers had underworld connections, and I envisioned that the scribbling on the slip said something like, "You take all of Detroit and give me Harlem".

When I delivered phone call notices to the professional gamblers, I always got a tip in the form of a crisp dollar bill, as though it had been newly minted. Those weekend gigs gave me plenty of spending money. In fact, I was earning more than my father. My father, who received free housing, eggs and chickens, received a moderate salary. I sometimes earned as much as $100 a weekend. Although I would give most of it to my parents, the fact that it was all cash tips allowed me enough control to keep some for myself.

As my contributions to the house grew, so did my voice. I had an opinion about everything, and realized that I carried an inordinate amount of power in the family. I do not know what my father was like before the war, but I do know that his spirit was crushed by the physical and psychological pain he endured during the war and he never recovered from it. Reluctantly, he simply followed in my mother's footsteps. At the same time, my mother, became more and more an advocate for me, at my father's expense.

A breach formed between my father and I, the Oedipal Complex was in full bloom, as I competed for my mother's hand. I eclipsed my father's authority and became the center of our family. In fact, I despised my father and felt embarrassed by him. It was no wonder that he sought refuge in his 1955 second-hand Buick. The Buick, with its light green, plush leather seats, white wall tires and distinct three circular vents on either side of the hood, was cavernous and became his private space for escape.

My father spent more and more of his free time waxing and preening his big gleaming idol, while I filled the parental void as the disciplinarian and guardian of my sister. I saw my father as a weakling and I aspired to be different and stronger. I understood that in this country, money was all powerful and worshiped as the "true" religion. It was through those narrow lenses that I measured and analyzed people and the world around me, and my moral compass became further obscured.

Besides the role of financial supporter, I took on the roles of advocate and cheerleader. As a confidante and counselor, I not only advised my parents, but also became their representative when it was necessary to communicate with the outside world.

My English language skills were quite good, while my parents remained much more comfortable speaking in their native tongue. As cheerleaders, Marja and I performed for the amusement of our parents. Usually these were slapstick routines like Sid Caesar and Imogene Coca or Charlie Chaplin. We felt obliged to keep our parents' spirits up, to console them, to shield them from harm, and to absorb their anguish.

The more I played these other roles, the more they distorted my own floundering identity. What happened to that little boy who grew into a teenager, whose sense of self free floated between the ages of ten and twenty-five? How old was he really? Who was guiding him; who had his back? Where were the role models? There were no trusted elders to seek counsel, or to bounce ideas off. There were no echoes, no responses, just the grinding of teeth at night.

13

My parents received a letter from the Dijkstra family that jolted me and sent me into a state of mourning for several weeks. Moeder had died. My parents had kept up a correspondence with the Dijkstra's, but I rarely thought of Moeder. This was the "mother" who cared for me from my infancy until age three, but I had not directly connected with her for over twelve years.

Whether I had attempted to erase her from my memory or hide her in a small black box deep within me, it didn't seem to matter. My tears flowed nonstop for weeks, and I could not be consoled by my parents.

Rationally, I could not understand why a person no longer central in my life for so many years had such a profound impact on me. Her place in my heart, along with the grief of that separation, was deeply stored away until the sudden and stark news of her death. My crumpled memories of her, like faded black and white photographs, fused together, formed a picture of a strong, modest and quietly loving woman who fiercely protected me.

Though I was nearly sixteen, I continued to emotionally waddle like the toddler I was in her care. But, her love and acceptance in my early years provided a cushion against all the sharp edges that were to come.

I basically drifted through high school and life without a footprint. I was simply air that was framed by a body and thus floated above, without any apparent impact on anyone or anything. My music teacher signed my senior yearbook and noted that I was the "happy wanderer".

My forced happiness was simply a shield that belied how I truly felt. When friends asked me what my plans were after graduation, I gave the standard response of, "probably college".

Most other students had a plan or at least a plan devised for them by their parents. I didn't have anyone to follow or to provide me with any direction. My parents hoped that I would find work, take care of myself, and if I went to college, that would be a bonus.

Unlike most teens, there was no parental authority, or advice to inspire me to go in one direction or another. At the same time, I had perfected the "aura" that I knew what I was doing and didn't need help from anyone. It was all a charade, a mask to hide my vulnerability, insecurity, and the anger of a crying child.

It seemed that my graduation and my parents' interest in returning to New York City were a coincidence. But, my parents (especially my mother) were upset about the farm owners not fulfilling their promise of buying a separate house for my family. The house to be was a few miles away from the farm, near an old cemetery. But, for one reason or another Bob and Martin kept delaying the purchase.

Concurrently, my parents talked about moving closer to the family and consciously planned to do so when I graduated. They felt that the timing worked for Marja as well, since she had just finished eighth grade and could more easily adapt to a new school environment. However, any change, even if it's for the better, had to be absorbed, and that wasn't the case.

Neither Marja nor I were ready for another move, and it created emotional turmoil for both of us. It was June 1960 when the family moved back to Rockaway Park, but I happily had a reprieve due to my summer work at the Concord Hotel.

PART 4

AMERICA 1960 - 1977

14

There was a stark contrast between the opulence of the Concord Hotel and the spartan workers' quarters where I lived with two other employees. A service road separated these bungalows from the hotel like a body of water separating two distinct islands. I was the Page captain, which gave me some authority in addition to a base salary. Whereas I dutifully sent the small base salary to my parents, I kept all the tips.

Hustling became second nature to me. Nightly, I would host card games in my bungalow, provide refreshments and charge a "cut" for each game played. During the day, I provided room service before the bar opened and wrote up the bar checks, payment that I pocketed completely, instead of just keeping the tip.

As the Page captain, I was the focal point for many requests and had the pageboy staff to fulfill my dictums. I coordinated various concessions from flower delivery to luggage pick up (by always stashing a rack in the guest's closet) to sharing information about the whore house on Liberty Street in Monticello. For each concession, I got a kickback from the pages who fulfilled the task.

Every night, after hosting the card games, I reentered the hotel and either hung out in the Night Owl Lounge, where a jazz trio performed or checked out what was happening in the night club. I wore "sharp duds", like a sport jacket with hidden buttons (just like O.C. Smith, the resident blues singer) and splashed on a cologne called Canoe to all discrete parts of my body. I was living the dream, and felt like Mr. Cool.

With no guidance from my parents, I thought of becoming an actor. I had never read a script or performed in a school play, but my boundless need for recognition and empathy made acting an easy choice. Besides, I was very impressed by Cary Grant, and like so many others, attempted to mimic his film voice. My sister was very enthusiastic about the idea, but my parents were not supportive. Although I auditioned (part of the admissions' process) for The American Academy of Dramatic Arts, I lacked confidence and never completed the application process.

We initially moved back to the same house and basement apartment where we had lived in after our stay at Tante Judith's house. Once my father found work in the garment Industry, we moved to Far Rockaway, to a two-bedroom apartment in a new building along Mott Avenue.

Marja and I shared a bedroom, which meant that if one of us wanted privacy the bathroom became the sanctuary. After a sublime summer at the Concord, this new setting meant that I was reentering my parents' world, with their dreams and nightmares, and it was difficult to adjust.

It was both desolate and familiar, a dark stifling narrow hall where I could neither find my way nor see myself. Marja had difficulties in school and was more preoccupied with her boyfriend than anything else.

In retrospect, I realized that she too was trying to leave the house, eager to create her own life and world through the cultivation of her burgeoning relationship. I wanted to live on my own, but felt compelled to help my parents, as they had done for their own parents. I felt enslaved.

In the fall of 1960, I got my first adult job on Gates Avenue in Flushing, Queens where I worked as an assistant bookkeeper for a small office furniture company. Every day, I walked between rows of six-foot high grey metal cabinets and black four-drawer extra deep file cabinets. At the end of this industrial setting was my grey metal desk, grey swivel cushioned chair, plus an assortment of oversized ledger binders, accounting worksheets, pencils and a large adding machine. Their collective size dwarfed my spirit and left just enough space for the typewriter.

The subway trip to work was long, made longer by the usual delay at Broad Channel Drive. The endlessly long subway ride, cold or hot depending on the season, the meaningless work, listening to the nervous grunts of my boss clearing his throat, and the fast food lunches that inflamed my stomach, all combined to form a daily hell.

Three evenings a week I attended Brooklyn College, excelling in Accounting, but little else. I was neither prepared for college, nor had the ambition and discipline to do well-and for what? I had no vision of the future.

I struggled to create a separate psychological space for myself, and endured my parents' lament that I was selfish for not wanting to do what they expected. Again, their words stung and reverberated within, but I did not give in to their wishes. I really didn't know what I wanted to do, but I knew I didn't like my life as it was.

On free evenings (mostly on weekends) I walked aimlessly on the boardwalk. The mist and the yellow lights of ancient street lamps combined to create long shadows and mystery. I hoped my shadow would point to a girl who could peer into my soul, fulfil my desire and cradle me.

Here and there I found someone equally fragile. We dated a few times, kissed and fondled on park benches, and then we each slipped away into the night. No phone numbers were exchanged, no roots were formed and no promises were made. There were no tomorrows. Today it would be called a modified hook up. This social experience seemed more masturbatory than real, and was barely three-dimensional.

My father went back to work in a familiar environment, the garment industry. He had worked for a similar factory in 1954, but it seemed more challenging this time around. He was older now, and he missed the work on the chicken farm and the serenity and solitude he found in the Gilboa valley in Israel.

He now spent his work days loading an assortment of dresses, suits and outerwear on large racks, then pushing these racks and hauling them onto open trucks. The grime of the city, the snow, and the summer heat were a dismal contrast to the farm and kibbutz.

He gained no satisfaction from this work, because it was dehumanizing. He received no recognition. He was just a pair of hands moving racks, veins bulging at the neck, muscles straining, spliced with the occasional denigrating joke of a fellow worker. He could not wait to get home after work, to eat my mother's cooking, to have a cigar, watch TV, fall asleep, and somehow wake up exactly when the following day's weather was broadcast on the eleven o'clock news. The drudgery of his work life was only softened by the vibrancy and comfort of his 1955 Buick.

Every Friday, my parents would see the rest of the family. That is, the Trompetter family including cousins Jack and Andy's parents, and my father's brother Jules and Emmy. All told there were three Trompetter families (made up of the three brothers, Gerrit, Joel, Moritz and respective spouses) two Gosler families and Jan and Corrie for a total of twelve. They either met in Beach Haven where the Trompetters, and Jan and Corrie lived, or Rockaway where my parents lived, or Brooklyn where Jules and Emmy lived.

The families looked forward to socializing with one another after a hard week of work, but it would often be tumultuous as well. We called it the "Friday Night Fights", a play on the Gillette razor sponsored boxing matches that aired each Friday evening.

The get-together would become more boisterous as scotch and soda or highballs made of Dutch gin and tonic were imbibed. Often there were political arguments, followed by teasing. They had survived the war, shared horrific experiences and fueled by alcohol, they became like children. They lost their inhibitions, and sometimes reverted to petty verbal attacks and bitter criticism.

My father, who had less formal education was very patriotic and more conservative than the others. He was often teased for his straight-laced political ideas and love of everything American. At the end of the evening, each kissed the other good night, but few left without some invisible scars.

The advertising jingle, "See the USA, in your Chevrolet...", stuck in my mind for many years. It wasn't so much the brand, as the vision of free movement, flight and control.

The hopelessly long trip to Flushing, followed by evenings at Brooklyn College, prompted me to ask my father for money to buy a car.

Much to my surprise, he agreed to lend me up to a thousand dollars. I had already passed my driver's license test by practicing at the Reese Park parking lot, and was thrilled when my father and I bought a used 1960 Dodge convertible with a push button automatic shift. I navigated the narrow toll lanes at the Marine Parkway Bridge and learned to bob and weave and slither between the double-parked cars in the Midwood section near Brooklyn College.

I felt uplifted by the car, remembering how sweet it was cruising in Marc's car up and down Broadway in Monticello. It made it easier to see my cousins, Andy and Jack, in Beach Haven, and later in Brooklyn Heights. That piece of property on wheels made me proud, just as my father felt with his first car and it embellished my social life.

No longer was heavy petting restricted to park benches, movie theaters or under the boardwalk, I now had the privacy of a car. It was at about this time that I met my first bona fide girlfriend, Lois. It was a serious relationship, but I felt more and more constricted by it, mostly due to her or her parents' conventional expectations of a job, responsibilities, home and children. The relationship felt boring, lifeless and finite, and I was much relieved when she broke it off during her first year at college.

It wasn't long thereafter that I met Susan, a Jewish policeman's daughter, and heavy petting flowered into something more. Susan and I visited the chicken farm where I grew up, chitchatted with Martin and walked around the farmstead.

The passage of time can be ruthless, even though fewer than three years had passed, the place had lost its luster. We went for a stroll through the fields and I showed her where I picked wild blueberries. Sitting under an old apple tree, the field grasses were soft to the touch as we crumpled to the ground and caressed. It took a while for me to get hard; I felt nervous and awkward. This was new to me. We stayed there for a while, our bodies warm from the sun and passion. Afterwards, I inhaled the cigarette smoke with an air of contentment I had not felt before.

It was 1963. I was now twenty-one and wanted to leave home more than ever, but my life was further complicated by the military draft. At age eighteen I filed for a 3-A hardship exemption. Every year thereafter I had to prove that the deferment was still valid.

I gave half of my income to my parents and their standard of living would have been profoundly impacted if I no longer supported them. I was concerned that if I left my parents' home it might be more difficult to prove that I was still supporting them. The Vietnam War was escalating, and I stayed home a little longer to maintain my deferment. My mother was adamant about not allowing me to be drafted, declaring, "If we have to, we'll move to Canada." She was not going to lose another loved one, especially her son, to war. I understood her resolve, but didn't fully believe she would go through with it, nor would I be thrilled to move yet again.

Later that year, cousin Jack moved out of the flat he shared with Andy, and I seized the opportunity to leave my parents' home and take Jack's place at Andy's flat. Fortunately, the Selective Service Board did not dictate that individuals with Hardship Exemptions needed to reside in the same home as the intended beneficiaries.

Thus, I just simply had to prove through annual audit visits that I continued to give half of my income to my parents. Although I was young and did not have a clear political perspective, I experienced the scars of war and developed a healthy skepticism about its need or sanity. This had nothing to do with defending your own home. This aimless war simply could get you killed.

15

Cousin Andy lived on Henry Street in Brooklyn Heights, in a fourth-floor walkup, facing the front of the building. It was a railroad flat, with one small room folding into another. There was a Murphy Bed in the front room and a fire escape partially blocking the view out of one window.

Andy and Jack were also hidden during the WWII, each separately, but their wartime experiences were difficult and painful compared to mine. Andy's parents were murdered during the war, and Jack shifted from one underground family to another. He was one of a number of children hidden and had to compete for attention, affection and nourishment.

I, on the other hand, was loved and nestled with a single family for the duration of the war, and became part of their family.

Andy, four months older than us, was the least mature, had boundless creativity and no doubt due the loss of his parents, was the most troubled. Tall, stocky, and barrel-chested, with curly light brown hair, he exuded warmth and charisma. He chain-smoked, ate and drank voraciously, ignoring doctors' orders, and sadly died in 1979 at the age of 37.

By the time I moved into the apartment on Henry Street, Andy was already involved with the Bread and Puppet Theater, had developed an aesthetic and political vision, and had a rebellious and sullen streak about him that impressed me. But, it was his laughter, which filled the air with euphoria, that attracted me the most. I felt I was entering a new world and that Andy, like Moses, would show me the way.

I was now working at a small family company that manufactured and serviced sub-pumps. As the "senior accountant", I was a full-charge bookkeeper and had three clerks reporting to me. My wages had increased and I looked up to my boss, the treasurer, a man I respected and who treated me as a son.

The fact that I was recognized as part of management did not stop me from privately talking to the workers in the shop and encouraging them to voice their displeasure over their wages and working conditions. The family-owned company was not unionized and I hoped that the collective bargaining option would help them move forward.

The distance between my new "digs" and my parents' home meant that instead of outright hostility towards my dad, we now had an understanding of sorts. But, it would still be quite a few years before I could understand what that historical acrimony was all about, learn to bridge that gap, form a healthy relationship with him, and even meet for drinks.

Although my new job was more interesting than the one in Flushing, it was still a job, and I felt stuck. At the same time, I shifted from a world of black and white to a world of color. It was as though I had been asleep for many years and awakened to a world that was bright, filled with streams of energy and always on the "go".

Following in Andy's footsteps I slowly went off the main political highway and promptly found a variety of dirt roads filled with new people and new ideas. I embraced anarchism, experimented with psychedelic drugs and read prodigiously. It didn't matter whether it was pseudo or a real change. What mattered was that it was a change. Sometimes change for its own sake has value, and it certainly gave me the psychological space to explore both the world around me, and the remote recesses of my mind.

The Bread and Puppet Theater, a people's theater, started by Peter Schumann, was steeped in the medieval tapestry of religious Passion Plays, combined with slapstick, parody and political satire. They were performing at St. Mary's Park in the south Bronx, and Andy invited me to join him.

The theater group, made up of a half a dozen dedicated performers and many part-time volunteers was setting up to perform in a small vest-pocket park. There was a dragonhead the size of a Volkswagen Beetle and a bright green train of fabric for the body that must have extended fifty feet. A strong wind rippled the fabric, while underneath a sea of children's sneakers marched slowly forward down the street.

To animate the dragon even more, smoke was bellowing out of its nostrils. Adults wearing all black, with gruff white skull masks helped-out or played flutes and drums. It was a surreal procession, accompanied by children's laughter, moving slowly on the cracked sidewalks strewn with garbage. Everywhere there where growing numbers of curious onlookers.

This gathering of children, the dragon, and the community was intoxicating. I inhaled it all. It rekindled the sensations I felt as a child when I performed for my sister with hand and finger puppets or the thrill I felt watching Punch and Judy at Christmas in Holland. It wasn't long thereafter that I volunteered with the Bread and Puppet Theater on a part-time basis.

A coarse, chewy, sour dough pumpernickel bread was always handed out, sometimes during or after a Bread and Puppet performance. There was a delicate balance between Peter's vision and the collaboration of the group. Digging clay from the pits, shaping and making puppets and writing the scripts and skits gave me a sense of meaning I had not felt since I was a child in Beit HaShita.

I loved the vaudevillian form of marketing, hawking Bread and Puppet newsletters, shouting, "One for a dime and two for a quarter." The baking of bread and other such tasks, were done collectively and added to my sense of community and purpose.

Peter and his wife, Elka, the wise and strong earth-mother, became for me the ideal parents I never had. My part-time involvement with this neo-communal theater group during the mid to late 1960s also showed how effectively theater can be introduced into anti-war and civil rights demonstrations.

16

In the summer of 1963, Andy and I travelled to Northern Europe, specifically Holland, Germany and Denmark. Our Icelandic flight landed in Luxembourg and from there we hitched and travelled by train through Germany and then Holland. It was interesting that in Germany there was a clear fault line between the young and old. We stayed at the University of Münster in northern Westphalia and found that many of the students were guilt ridden about WWII.

There was a definite schism between young adults and their parents, who either participated in the War effort directly or simply tolerated what was happening around them. The adults believed that they were fulfilling their patriotic duty, while their children felt alienated and guilty about the war, their country and their parents' participation.

There was a fault line of sorts in me as well. By this time, I no longer blamed or felt hatred towards Germany and the German people for what happened to me and my family, and by extension to six million Jews. On the other hand, I could never forgive or forget. The concept of forgiveness, for me, works in relation to individuals, like my parents, or a friend, but to forgive a nation and its people for the horrors committed would be beyond comprehension.

When we arrived in Holland we first visited relatives, then Vader in Wageningen. I had not seen or spoken to him in over sixteen years. His face, stern as ever, was made softer by his smile and greetings.

Vader had remarried and was living in a different neighborhood. He and I took a stroll in our old neighborhood and into the inner city. Strolling in the town, Vader asked neighbors and shopkeepers whether they knew that the young child living with them was Jewish. Many replied that they did, while a few were surprised.

One neighbor, who had hidden a Jewish teenager during the war, when food was scarce, periodically gave the Dijkstra family an extra food ration book just to make sure that I had enough to eat.

Andy and I spent two nights with Vader reminiscing about my childhood in Wageningen, but mostly he wanted to hear about my life now, my parents and my sister. I tried to gloss over the forty-eight hours I spent with Vader, hiding the heaviness in my throat and chest. All sorts of feelings and images sprouted like weeds after a heavy rain. The cobble stones were still the same, but everything else had changed.

For me, the old house and neighborhood were frozen in time, like my heart and memories. We did not talk much about the past, and at the time I was glad he didn't, but each word he did utter felt like a communion ritual, and for a brief time I was home.

Though many years had passed, my sense was that he loved me and was proud of me. As we left to hitchhike elsewhere, Andy and I noticed Vader and his new wife standing on their porch, waving farewell to us. Butterflies fluttered in my stomach and my throat tightened, knowing I would never see him again.

A day later we had lunch with Vader's oldest daughter, Anneke, who had married and had a young child named Caroline. Playing a child's game with Caroline and picking cherries together from the trees behind their house diminished the anguish I felt. I would continue to see and correspond with Anneke for decades thereafter.

Sometimes she would visit us in New York City and at other times we would visit her in Holland. For me, it was always a moving experience. I felt so lucky to know her. She was a direct link to my infancy and her presence and her memories stretched the boundaries of my life. But she was more than that, she was my older sister!

Andy and I also visited relatives and friends in Amsterdam and Tilburg, and then travelled to Copenhagen. It was on our adventure to Denmark that Andy and I mimicked a page out of the "prankster playbook" when we stripped to our underwear in the 3rd class cabin of our train.

We reasoned that no other passengers would feel comfortable being there with two half-naked men. Sure enough, two middle-aged women knocked on the sliding doors, saw us in our near nakedness, took a step back and disappeared. As a result, Andy and I had the cabin to ourselves from Hamburg to Copenhagen. We could stretch out and sleep, each on our own cushioned bench for the five plus hours the trip took.

Three days later, while back in Hamburg, for our amusement, we followed a man who looked like the prototypical SS officer. He wore a black double-breasted leather coat with black storm trooper boots, and except for the Panama hat, could have easily passed for a German officer.

Andy and I were drinking a codeine-laced cough medicine that we bought over-the-counter and we were slowly getting high. The escapade was like a scene out of a movie, especially when the man took a drag on a cigarette, holding it between thumb and index finger. Giddy and high, I was not angry at what this man represented, instead we laughed hysterically. These were the years for self-development and for escape. I needed to process who I thought I was before I could handle the pain of my distant past. I did not realize at the time that the two were intertwined.

On another occasion, in Amsterdam, we walked with a group of long-haired people, led by someone who looked distinctly like Dave van Ronk, singing folk songs in the Red-Light District. We were asking for loose change from the prostitutes, who sat in windows and lined the doorways, but only one responded, "Ik heb geen cent in mijn kut". Loosely translated as, "I don't have a cent in my ass".

17

These were carefree days that continued even when we returned to Brooklyn Heights. We each bought a scooter, Andy a Vespa and I a Cushman. The latter looked more like a dwarfed motorcycle, because it had very wide, rough, scooter-size tires and had a stick shift. I remember crossing the Brooklyn Bridge, flying high, and going sixty miles per hour, with Andy on his Vespa, singing, "Hallelujah I'm Bum," an old Wobblies' folk song.

Each new experience whether that of participating in an eight-millimeter film, performing with the Bread and Puppet Theater or travelling, uncovered a host of sensations that attacked my nervous system. This was especially true of the latter.

Traveling in Europe was a new experience for me. I was both exhilarated and frightened by the experience. I realized that I could not tolerate extremes, and when possible, made sure to remain in familiar environments or wherever I felt some control. I could tolerate neither highs nor lows because if I did, I feared I would fall apart.

Only on rare occasions, possibly when the sun, moon and stars were aligned just perfectly, I would let go and float in the wind aimlessly, like a fallen leaf. These states sometimes came about naturally, but were also chemically induced through drugs or alcohol.

The foundation of trust and assurance of safety, that are necessary for anyone who wanders out of the cave, would take many, many years to form before I could feel comfortable in the playpen called the universe. However, the freedom experienced when physically traveling did awaken a need for inward travel as well, and my life began to slowly change course.

Not only did each experience percolating within me bring up new ideas and feelings, but also the public arena, the polis became important. I joined the picket lines at the NYS Supreme Court, marches at the Pentagon, marches in support of the Viet Cong, and rallies at the U.N. or Columbia University.

Each event further convinced me of the great disparity between white America and everyone else. Whether it occurred through Machiavellian calculation, apathy or sheer stupidity, I could no longer tolerate inaction. I realized that the countless marches and rallies impacted me immediately, while the rest of America might be impacted later, or not at all. It didn't matter, I felt that I could not be a spectator and in many ways demonstrated not only for equality, peace and freedom, but also for those who did not act or were murdered during WWII.

Like my father, I too wanted to shed my past, to lose my accent, to "fit in", but the political and cultural waves of the 1960s, and my awakening consciousness, dictated that I take a different, possibly, longer path.

I looked forward to no longer having a job, or being responsible for my parents' welfare. I needed the freedom to experiment, and to act as I chose to, differently than I ever had before. Joining the picket lines and various marches allowed me to act in a public way for the first time. I was being spontaneous, taking risks and ownership of ideas and beliefs, and in a way, I was no longer consciously hiding.

The civil rights and anti-war movements for me were about siding with the oppressed, and making things right. My wish to see Israel again changed as I became aware of the similarities between Israel's domestic policies towards its own Arab and Palestinian citizens and the governmental apartheid in South Africa or the treatment of black people in this country.

The United States' policy to support a puppet dictator in Vietnam against the will of its people further highlighted for me how governments anywhere can selectively support or oppress people. My animosity towards Israel seemed to grow in tandem with US policies in Vietnam. I always found it contradictory for people to support civil rights in this country and be pro-Israel at the same time.

I now recognized that the Zionism that was fostered on the kibbutz, and which I cherished as a child, came at the expense of the Palestinians in the form of lives, land and culture. I was embarrassed that Jews especially (People of the Book) could behave in this manner, since I had always believed that Jews were taught ethics and had a moral compass.

It taught me an important lesson. Every person or country has the capacity to be both a victim and a perpetrator, sometimes at the same time. This sad conflict between supporting what is ethically right and a longing to see where I grew up, to touch the soil and to see the Jezreel Valley from the Gilboa, has been gnawing at my heart for a long time.

18

On the Friday afternoon, November 22nd, the news of President Kennedy's assassination was a shock and an awakening. This terrible news was like a gigantic wave that buried the 1950s and simultaneously brought to the surface a new age. The Eisenhower period with its robust economy, typified by mass production of automobiles and the thruway, Wonder Bread and TV shows like "Father Knows Best", had lulled the American people into believing that their world was homogeneous and safe.

The tucked-away communities, where everyone and everything mirrored themselves, was jolted into a new reality. The dreams of people who endured two wars, WWII and the Korean War, were no longer shared by their children. A chasm had formed, with younger people on one side and older people on the other. The former wished to go back to the earth, believed in tolerance and diversity, while the latter craved safety, uniformity and comfort.

The social fabric had been tearing for quite a while and this divide culminated in a lack of trust between generations. It was on this solemn Friday evening that my friend and I walked on Bleecker

Street, while police on horseback, in riot gear, waited for the unexpected.

While I was struggling to find my own path, my sister was moving in her own direction. She was alienated by her new environment in Far Rockaway and as a result struggled through high school. Although she was born after the war, Marja had absorbed my parents' angst to such an extent that she took on the role of both messenger and caretaker.

Like Mercury, she oscillated between them and me, bringing news from one to the other, and back. As a caretaker, she nurtured and sustained our parents' wounded spirits. She was bound to them in such a way that it stifled her own development. As a teenager of fifteen she found salvation in "going steady". She started dating a boy one year older than herself, and no doubt hoped to create her own life, separate and distinct from the world in which she was mired. Irwin and Marja married four years later, and moved to Belle Harbor to create their own nest.

Although I enjoyed my job, it became secondary to my political and aesthetic vision and at some point, it weighed on me like an albatross. My focus was changing. The empire-building stage of my life was no longer important. I wanted to expand my horizons and narrow my expenses. That would give me the ability to work part time and allow me to fit more comfortably into my new proletarian vision.

I sold whatever stocks I owned, sold my car, quit my job and moved to a tenement flat on the Lower East Side, a fourth-floor rent-controlled walkup. I built a bed using a sheet of plywood that rested on top of four wooden milk crates that I found on the street. The milk crates also served as mini bookcases. I purchased a foam mattress, a soft pillow and some kitchen equipment.

The apartment was a long corridor space with two working fireplaces and a bath / shower unit in the kitchenette. The change in lifestyle and the low rent allowed me to take either part-time or seasonal work and offered me the freedom to do what I wanted.

My only concern was the Draft and I gambled that since I was nearing 26 the Draft Board would no longer be interested in me and would look for younger candidates. Fortunately I was right, and concurrently my parents were earning more income.

My mother, for the first time since working as a beautician in Holland before the war, began to work at W.T. Grant Stores. The store clerk job truly energized and empowered her, connected her to other people, and inspired her to march for peace with other women. Work for my mother was a gateway towards self-actualization. Her memory of this time helped her flower into a vibrant person, as she got older.

The 1960s allowed me the freedom of movement to create a psychological distance from all the outside forces that undermined my growth: my parents, full time employment, high rent and other responsibilities.

This escapism gave me the time to begin to understand who I was and who I wanted to become. These were adventurous times for me. I was like a fruit fly, at times glued to the ripened fruit and at times hovering above it, perpetually busy and hungry. I felt I belonged for the first time, not unlike how I felt on the kibbutz.

Like many of my new friends I let my hair grow longer and sported a wild mustache. The pendulum had swung from right to left, from what is to what ought to be, and that meant that all that I was, was no longer. It also meant that I distanced myself as much as I could from my parents and their way of life.

As a result, I rarely attended family celebrations such as birthdays, holidays and picnics. I needed to sever the emotional umbilical cord. All my conscious life I felt total bondage to my parents and felt the burden of having to shield them from potential harm. I wanted to diffuse the pain that enveloped them. It is no wonder that without hesitancy, I shared my income with them. Over time, that fealty distorted my views on work and what it meant to be responsible for or to someone.

On the other hand, I did form a new relationship with my father. The physical distance between us allowed me to see my father in a new light. He came over to my flat a couple of times and we went out for a beer.

On one such occasion, while we both were relieving ourselves in a bathroom, I was shocked to see that my pop had a normal-sized penis. For years, I was convinced that the image I had of my father correlated with a smaller than usual sized penis.

On another occasion, I realized that deep within his emotional scar tissue beat a young heart. My father shared with me that he always saw himself as an artist and that he pictured himself living on an island off the Grecian coast, not disturbed by anything, just focused on his painting.

As I began to be at peace with my father, I no longer felt embarrassed by him, although I could never accept him as a role model. I was maturing.

Living by myself on the Lower East Side, paying $38 a month rent, meant that for the first time I was beating my own drum. I shared my tenement flat with "Black Ike", a sweet furry cat, born on the day Eisenhower died. On the fourth floor I lived across from Pharoah Sanders, a tenor saxophonist, who had just left the John Coltrane Band to make his own way in the jazz world.

For my own pleasure, I took up the C-flute, but mostly played on wooden and bamboo flutes. I was impressed by Yusef Lateef, a popular jazz flute player, and how he played the bamboo flute to make the sheep-like bleating sounds. I never learned notes, nor was I a good player, but from time to time my sound was pure and meshed well with Sanders' practice notes next door. In fact, Pharoah Sanders, quiet as ever, mumbled something about my sound being good when he exited his apartment, as I left mine.

I had a ravenous appetite (a Gosler tradition) and, like my father, hated to wait for food to be ready. If I was hungry my mood could change in a nanosecond from Clark Kent into a werewolf. Fortunately, I enjoy cooking and became a good cook. This seemed just right, since dependency on others for anything, was akin to being controlled. Chicken was my specialty and I would make *arroz con pollo*, paella or grilled chicken on the hibachi that I put on my fire-escape.

Early on I realized that cooking nurtured me. I think my reverence for food, cooking, eating and sharing was central to who I am. My family gathering for the evening meal with its intimacy and warmth, insulated me from anxiety and gave me the illusion that everything was and would be ok.

My ability to cook was also a feather in my cap when it came to attracting women. In calculated fashion, I would ask my date whether she was hungry, and if she said, "yes", I would say, "Well, let me make you a chicken or pasta dish or something". Inevitably, that impressed her. It must be true that the way to a woman's heart is through her stomach.

I was dating a lot and often different women at the same time. On occasion, I would form relationships that lasted six months to a year, but mostly they were short lived. However, unlike the internet generation, once the relationship ended—whether it lasted a week or a year—I no longer communicated with that person. The idea of continuing a non-sexual relationship was not part of the 1960s, at least not for me.

It was 1968. To pay the rent I had seasonal work, such as wrapping packaging at Bloomingdale's during the Christmas holidays, selling marijuana, or selling assemblages made with plaster, fur, seashells and brillo pads.

Andy gave me the confidence to make these pieces, but I never sold many. I also worked at a two-year commercial college for six weeks. The school targeted primarily poor students and promised them good jobs at the end of the two-year program. Since most of the students came from families who lived below the poverty level, the school thrived on the subsidies they received from federal and state agencies.

I quit after six weeks because of an incident that happened with a fellow worker. I didn't like how the owner of the school treated him. He toyed with the guy—for no reason at all—and made him into his whipping boy. I felt awkward and furious at the same time and told the owner that unless he treated all employees fairly I would quit. This seemed to impress rather than anger the boss and he offered me a raise to stay. Money never drove me one way or another, but I saw the writing on the wall and quit that same afternoon.

Although this incident differed from the warning I received in Israel about Ahmed, the parallels were clear. Once again, a powerful person was belittling someone who was vulnerable. As a Jew and a victim of the war, I identified strongly with those at risk and the oppressed.

With no vision nor ambition, my experience at Brooklyn College was dismal. It seemed that the F grade was specifically designed for me. I was expelled and went to a community college, where I did quite well. I then re-enrolled at Brooklyn College where my grades improved but not as quickly as they liked.

As a result, I re-enrolled at NYC Community College where I met Raul. We had many things in common: we liked to write, enjoyed films and film making, had patched together academic goals for ourselves, and loved to fantasize about the future while we smoked pot. Often, we rode on the Myrtle Avenue El to his mother's apartment in oppressive heat, sitting on the straw-covered seats, chatting about our poetry or short story writings.

We plotted all sorts of ways to make money, schemes that could only be hatched while in an altered state. Raul was seeing someone at that time, and they were getting quite serious. In fact, she gave birth to a son, whom they named Christian. The sweet baby changed the nature of our relationship. Although we continued to get high together, the change came simply because Raul was focused on his family.

At the same time, I wondered whether to start a serious relationship myself. Not only did I believe that I lacked the maturity, but, intuitively, I believed that children and drugs didn't mix. I stayed in touch with Raul on and off for quite a while, and then we no longer crossed paths.

With no ongoing work commitments or serious relationships to restrict me, I paid more attention to my college classes and enrolled at Richmond College, an experimental senior community college in Staten Island. I had changed my major from accounting and economics to history and theater, and found the time to be a day student.

The fact that I worked part time meant that there was no economic constraint, and with no serious academic vision, I took as much time as needed to get my Baccalaureate. As a result, I amassed more than a hundred and seventy credits and didn't complete my BA until the late 1970s.

College was just another forum to meet people and share ideas. The cafeteria was the most important classroom; there I could be student, teacher, and guru. The latter was appropriate because I was beginning to form a social / political clique and—as I was now one of the elder statesmen on campus—my voice perhaps had more meaning.

This was a time when student boycotts, sit-ins and the taking over of college facilities was commonplace. A group of maybe twenty students, including myself, took over a part of the building that included the cafeteria and kitchen. Since we had planned it carefully, I had time to rent the film "Battle of Algiers", an Italian / Algerian-produced neo documentary about the revolution in Algeria.

Taking over the cafeteria was calculated as well, because it allowed us to cook and serve a meal of Arroz con Pollo for more than a hundred people, while we watched the inspirational film. Both the film and the event were a learning experience and heightened the students' understanding of the politics of war and specifically guerilla warfare. No one was penalized for the takeover.

The disruption, if anything, inspired a teach-in, and allowed students to viscerally comprehend what was happening in Vietnam, both to its people and to the US soldiers. I was saddened and guilt ridden whenever I saw a soldier. Many young men had enlisted out of a sense of patriotism or hoping to create a better life for themselves. The Draft primarily swallowed those who did not have a college exemption, mainly poor black and white kids.

Nineteen sixty-eight was a pivotal year for me politically. The civil rights and anti-war movements had recently merged and created waves of change that rippled through the counter culture. It was also a time when I began to understand the contradictions and the absurdity of life.

For example, when I went to Washington with friends to demonstrate at the steps of the Pentagon, many people on the bus were more concerned with how to get back to the buses later in the day, than focusing on the meaning of the protest. While many of the demonstrators were gassed and knocked down by riot police, an equal number of people were more concerned with deciding where to eat after the demonstration. Somehow, the urgency of finding one's way back and discussing the day's "event" over food and drink took precedence over the event itself.

Clearly many demonstrators were sincere about their participation, but there seemed to be a larger number who were titillated by the social quasi-political experience, and the actual purpose of the demonstration became secondary. Perhaps it was simply their way of processing their own fears and insecurities. I began to understand that dealing with people was complicated, often contradictory, and could not fit into neat little binary units.

For me, the road was wide open. Not only was I free to do whatever I wanted, with minor guilt or concern, I could wear any mask that suited me. Since my sense of self was buried so deep inside of me, it was easy to take on different personas. I could be whomever I wanted to be. I could be a free spirit like Zorba the Greek, the last of the buccaneers, a pipe-smoking intellectual, a guerilla theater performer, or a blues singer.

My freedom of movement and thoughts were like a narcotic. I had never experienced such sensations before, and at times it was frightening. Often, those moments correlated very closely with my drug intake. I smoked pot daily and my routines seemed to revolve around the activities associated with addiction. Like food, I always made sure to have some weed around, and if I didn't have any, then devised ways to get some.

In fact, psychologically, I became dependent on pot. I truly believed that I was not as vibrant and interesting unless I was high. Consequently, whenever I had plans to meet someone or to go to a party, I made sure to have a little buzz on before I left the house. The drug highs were the norm and they helped to lessen my anxiety. In retrospect, I was, "Mr. Nowhere Man", from the Beatles' "Yellow Submarine". I was going nowhere fast!

The Lower East Side was a quirky kaleidoscope of textures, colors and nationalities. There were remnants of Jewish and Italian immigrant life, of cobblestone-streets, and Ukrainian shops and restaurants. There were tenements everywhere, housing Latinos, artists, Beats, students and prostitutes.

Except for the narrow homes and canals, it could have been the Red Light District of Amsterdam. In a word, it was a universe unto itself and it was my universe. On Second Avenue between Ninth and Tenth Streets was the Metro, a furniture store where besides buying furniture, one could order hot chocolate, lounge on couches, play chess, or listen to Allen Ginsberg recite poetry. A half block further north, at St. Marks Church in the Bowery, jazz was played in the evenings amidst the old gravestones in the cemetery. Tompkins Square Park had demonstrations, music and the ever-present scent of cannabis and urine.

19

I lived in Manhattan, but for certain mundane tasks such as haircuts or dental appointments I returned to Far Rockaway, where my parents lived. Although separation from my parents and the normal conventions that governed their lives was paramount, I was not ready to sever the emotional umbilical cord completely. Like a three-year-old, I wanted my space in the playground, but still needed my parents' eye in the background. Returning to Far Rockaway, subconsciously, was the last vestige of connection to my former life with my parents.

On one occasion, I decided to have dinner at my parents' house and have a haircut with my usual barber. The simple haircutting ritual turned into a nightmare when I learned that the barber who had been cutting my hair for years had died. It takes a definite amount of time to train a barber, a Pavlovian process that requires being literal, giving large tips and compliments on a job well done, before the results are satisfactory.

On this occasion, the session was exacerbated by the fact that the new barber understood little English and was extremely arrogant.

The results were not pleasing and it was the last time I traveled to Far Rockaway for a haircut.

On my way to my parents' apartment after my haircut, a woman with two young children begged for money. I recognized that they were gypsies and was ready to walk on, but her persistence made me stop and listen to her story.

The vaudevillian tale was not new to me, but somehow it shifted my focus to her needs and away from my haircut woes. I bought her two shopping bags of groceries, thinking that to be a more responsible way of supporting her family than giving her cold cash. I knew that I was being fleeced, but I felt better and continued my pilgrimage to my parents' place.

As I neared their three-story apartment building, I looked back towards the subway station and was surprised to see my father jogging in my direction.

At first, I thought he was simply trying to catch up with me, but as he came closer I could see that his face was creased with anxiety and alienation. My father was running home, away from his daily hell. I crossed the street to avoid any awkwardness or embarrassment as he ran by, fear etched on his face. I arrived at the apartment a calculated five minutes later, and my father welcomed me with his warm brown eyes, as though nothing had transpired.

The transformation confounded me, but I easily understood the stress he felt in the outside world and the need to hide it from himself and from me.

My corridor of an apartment became a bus stop of sorts, where old and new friends visited, stayed, and then continued onto wherever they were going. My friend Richie returned from the Peace Corps in Thailand and stayed with me in June of 1968 when Robert Kennedy was assassinated.

We walked to Washington Square where crowds had gathered to

listen to heart-wrenching folk songs and to share in the communal grief. The murder of President Kennedy, Malcolm X, Martin Luther King and Robert Kennedy, and then the shootings at Kent State, represented a dagger that pierced the public spirit and tarnished hope itself. I was no longer interested in demonstrations and public forums to question and protest.

I, too, felt hopeless and detached. Whether calculated or not, there was a collective interest in escape and many people achieved it by rejecting political action and retreating within themselves. Stumbling across the many potholes of my own life's journey, I did not seem unique in this titanic shift. In fact, hiding within my own inner sanctum seemed quite normal.

Almost four years had passed since I had a conventional job, hopes or dreams. I was beginning to question, whether this new life was the right path. More and more I focused on travel, both internal and external. With Peyote, Mescaline and LSD, I felt the texture of my thoughts. I was transported into the world of the senses, and that high touched the twin peaks of delight and fear.

At times, the exact images and sensations were felt simultaneously by more than one person. On those rare occasions, like overlapping soap bubbles, the hallucinating few eagerly shared and analyzed their experience, while inadvertently causing the bubbles to disperse and float away. To listen to one's own heart, to a friend or stranger, requires the discipline of silence. This was an immense challenge for me. To sit still, to let go, to truly listen, required a foundation of trust that I had not developed.

From my early beginnings, danger and transience were my sole companions, they taught me to be watchful and hyper-vigilant. It undermined my ability to focus on anything but my own survival. Listening remains a slippery slope even today.

It was 1969 when I found a part-time bookkeeping job at Two Bridges Neighborhood Council. Two Bridges was an anti-poverty program devoted to housing and education for immigrants and African-Americans who lived in the China Town area. The immigrants were mostly from South East Asia and Latin America. They spoke little English, and needed support on every level, from language skills to housing, to finding employment, and to solving everyday problems. A settlement house with a myriad of services would have been more appropriate, but because Two Bridges was nearby and had several people who spoke Mandarin and Spanish, the program's staff were inclined to help them in whatever way possible, and well beyond their mandate, which only related to housing.

My role was to record the expenses and to fill out the monthly requisitions that became the source of funding from one month to the next. I creatively managed the funds in such a way that I was able to "balance the books" while squirreling away funds for other programs not mandated by the federal government, such as urgently needed classes to teach English and related work skills. Once, we used the money for an outing to the countryside for people who had never been outside of Manhattan.

Although it had been five years since I worked at a regular job and had a presumed direction to my life, I was still nibbling at the edges, and was still rudderless. What was I running from and where was I going? I didn't know. It was as though an inner voice instructed me to, "Stay off the main road!"

The beauty of working at a federal- or state-sponsored anti-poverty program, like Two Bridges, was that the program was dependent on funding. That meant that one didn't know from one year to the next whether the program would still be around.

As a result, the permanence of one's job was tenuous and flexible. Conversely, it allowed for a lot of free time, and I exploited that to the fullest. It was quite common for me to take a couple of months off and simply find a replacement to fill in while I was gone. It was with that in mind, that I decided to go camping in Maine with Andy and two Estonian women.

Once I found a replacement, I informed Susan, my supervisor / office manager of my plans to vacation for the next two months, and that I would leave in two weeks. Unbeknown to me at the time, she also planned to quit before my vacation.

I was determined not to allow anything to interfere with my summer plan, and when I met the new office manager, told her as much. Basically, I introduced myself, welcomed her, and described what I did. Almost in the same breath, I told her I was leaving for the summer, but that she shouldn't worry because I had found a replacement to fill in while I was away. This rather brief, but potentially disruptive introduction, made the new office manager wonder what I was all about and whether she could depend on me when I returned.

The trip itself was memorable. In my used Chevy Impala, Andy, the two Estonian women and I travelled up route 22 towards Maine. We camped at Booth Bay Harbor. It was dusk, the sky was streaked with orange, and ships' bells chimed to mark time, while we toasted the sunset with chilled Chablis and good food. I hoped the meal and the vision would last indefinitely, but the mosquitoes and gnats had other plans and we retired behind the mosquito nettings of our respective tents.

The following day we met Jack and a friend of his at Acadia National Park, and for a few days, in two cars, we travelled and shared meals together. Then the woman who was with me decided to travel with Jack, and the two camps went their separate ways. On the surface, we were all free spirits and whether it was a minuet or a game of musical chairs, in the social game of chance, I lost—and it stung.

I returned to Two Bridges disillusioned and angry, and became more engaged in the anti-poverty program and in my party life.

The interesting side effect of the federal anti-poverty industry was that—although it supported a variety of needs such as day care, Head Start, housing, work programs and youth programs—it inadvertently created growth opportunities for the neighborhood people who were hired as para-professionals. They were inspired by the program and many returned to school, obtained their GEDs and went on to college.

They were mostly women from poor and / or dysfunctional families, who became social workers, teachers, lawyers and nurses after working for Two Bridges. These women became the models and advocates for social change. They inspired others, including their own children, to go to college and become leaders in their communities. I admired their energy and optimism, but it engendered no positive impact on me.

I threw myself into my social life with a new appetite and became involved with two women at the same time. Concurrently, my supervisor told me that she expected me to spend more time at work. This was a new dictum. Until that time, I was free to schedule my hours as I pleased, providing the work was completed in a timely manner. This rigidity annoyed me and I voiced my frustration to my new boss, Sheila.

20

At first Sheila was somewhat tentative, if not reticent, but after a couple of months, her commitment, sincerity and tenacity became quite apparent. She had a degree in English literature and an Associate's degree in textile design, neither of which prepared her for an anti-poverty program. However, serving people does not require a college degree, just the discipline to listen, to be empathic and to get things done. She excelled as the office manager, but I could tell that life wasn't perfect for her, as she often stayed late. I worked part-time, and would arrive late in the afternoon, when most employees were preparing to go home, and was always surprised to find Sheila, a young married woman, still lingering around the office.

She had been married for nearly two years and was unhappy with her husband and her in-laws. All this I learned during an evening's walk, when I escorted her across the Brooklyn Bridge to her Park Slope doorstep.

Over the weeks that followed, I walked her home more than once, sharing intimate details about myself. I became aware that she had an interest in me and that I was attracted to her as well. However, whether out of some bourgeois or macho ethic, I decided that getting involved with another man's wife was not right. Several months later, Sheila left her husband and began seeing me.

A party at my house was where we first connected. I liked to make parties and loved cooking lasagna and roast chicken for my friends. At times, I left my party before it ended, because another party invite was more attractive, or I followed my heart to take someone home.

Sometime later, I would return to my place, to find it empty or on occasion, to find a couple making out. So, it was surprising that on this occasion I returned to find that one person remained, Sheila, who was tidying up the party mess. It was even more enticing when I realized that she was wearing my father's moth-eaten woolen blue bathrobe and nothing else. There were no explanations needed, words were not exchanged, her crooked smile revealed a world of desire, and she stayed with me throughout the night.

By this time, Sheila had moved to Thompson Street in Little Italy. A sixth floor, one bedroom, walk-up in an old building with beautiful marble floors in the hallway. Little Italy was an area of small groceries, bakeries, butcher shops, delicatessens, restaurants, and private clubs still protected by Italian crime families.

This meant that the neighborhood was safe and orderly and managed by coercion. You could leave your apartment unlocked, but might also witness a shopkeeper being harassed for protection money by two knuckle-faced goons. Every evening, a bakery truck would park at Thompson and Spring Streets, attracting people from all over the neighborhood. There was no fresh dough to be found in the truck, except for the hard cash that people bet on the numbers racket or Italian lottery, as it was known.

Often, we stayed at one another's flats, although we were each still dating other people. It was on one of those occasions that the "Big

Toe Tragedy" occurred. We had been dating for about five months and I was at Sheila's. I asked her if she had anything to drink, but she was not into wine or alcohol. She remembered that she had been given a bottle of rum and told me it was in an upper cabinet.

When I reached for the bottle on the top shelf of the cabinet, the wooden folding chair I was standing on collapsed and my right foot slithered down one of the legs of the chair. Standing on the kitchen floor, in my underwear, clutching the bottle and somewhat high, I stared at the large puddle of blood that was accruing next to my foot. Perplexed as to what had happened, Sheila quickly found a white towel that she compressed on the side of the middle toe, stopping the bleeding and taped the two toes together. At the same time, I, with a forced casualness said, "Don't worry, I always bleed a lot". Somehow, it didn't bleed any further when we went to bed that night. However, as soon as I stood up the following day, the toe, tightly wrapped with the tape, started bleeding again. Now, we became alarmed and Sheila called 911 for an ambulance, telling them, "My friend has been cut!" She gave her address, but in the rush of it all, had not given the vital details such as how I was cut or what part of my body was bleeding.

A short time thereafter, two corpulent cops, huffing and puffing, with drawn guns, knocked on the door, only to find that my toe had been cut. Seeing that I was neither stabbed nor truly disabled, they asked if I could walk on my own. As soon as I took a single step, they could see that I was leaving a blood trail, and they decided, with my appreciation, to have me sit on a portable canvas seat. I put my arms around their round shoulders, while they lugged me down the stairs and into the waiting ambulance. Five minutes later, at St Vincent's emergency room, I was placed on a gurney in one of their corridors, and waited for their emergency care. A wild eyed, bare-chested man with lacerations all over his chest and upper arms walked by, and said, "So they got you too, eh?"

Throughout this time, Sheila was very concerned and attentive.

Ten minutes later my toe was sutured. It was only afterwards that we understood what had happened. I had severed the artery between the toes of my right foot. The fact that we didn't treat the wound more promptly, meant that I could have continued to bleed during the night, and certainly meant that there was a great possibility for infection. I was given antibiotics and told to remain horizontal for six weeks.

Marja lived in a comfortable rented house, near Belle Harbor in the Rockaways. She was a housewife kept busy by her toddler son, Steven, and a dutiful husband, Irwin, but she yearned for more. Upon hearing of my "toe tragedy", she invited me to recuperate at her house for as long as it took.

My sister had always taken care of me in times of need. She cherished me and her love bordered on adoration. I could not refuse. In retrospect, both Marja and I served each other not only as brother and sister, but also as surrogate parents. When I needed love and nurturing, Marja became my mother and nurse and when she needed a strong voice to back her up, I became her father and advisor. Clearly, neither role was perfectly acted out, but served us well, in the absence of our own parents' abilities to parent.

It came as no surprise, that I felt like a prince in her care. Marja provided me with food, comfort, and a modicum of adulation. I would entertain her with reports of my most recent exploits, my hopes, and aspirations and plans for travel. I also had visitors, including a girlfriend from Richmond College, several male friends and Sheila. In fact, Sheila visited on numerous occasions, which impressed me.

During my convalescence, Marja talked about her life, how she felt limited by it, and how she fantasized about doing so much more. I, the peacock, didn't think very highly of her husband, and supported her notion to spread her wings.

My existential description of freedom to be who you want to be, so

140

much a fabric of the times, resonated deeply with her own wishes, and she looked forward to the day when this would become her reality. In retrospect, I should have listened, been thankful to both hosts for their generosity, and kept my vision and opinions to myself. But, Marja had known my views well before, and I was too full of myself to understand their ultimate impact on her.

The time there passed quickly. I fell into a rhythm, spending my time reading, playing my wooden flutes and telling stories to my nephew.

21

By September of 1970, Sheila and I moved in together. In my tenement building, a large first-floor apartment opened and we took it in a heartbeat. The flat was above "Port of Call", a jazz bar. Periodically, we could hear the music wafting through the wooden floors. It was jazz and it was good. From our back windows we overlooked the old NYC Marble Cemetery, so called because of its underground marble burial vaults. The cemetery, with its high stone walls and pathways of grass in between the gravestones, gave me a sense of old New York and its bucolic past.

The apartment was a typical lower eastside flat consisting of two loft-like rooms connected to form a U-shaped apartment. The first room that you entered served as the kitchen with a slop sink, exposed brick wall and working fire place. The second room we used as a bedroom and in its center near the wall, free standing, was a claw foot tub. There was a separate closet-sized toilet nearby. The second room also had a slop sink and a working fire place. I built a wooden platform bed and heavy wooden shutters that functioned like window security guards. Being on the first floor meant easy access for potential intruders.

We also had two cats, Millicent and Black Ike. Millicent, Sheila's calico Maine Coon cat, seemed more human than feline, and continually defended her space against Ike, my stocky black furry bully. In some ways, they represented our respective needs, in that one feline needed her space, while the other needed nurturing and sex.

We planned to travel to Europe and North Africa, and full-time jobs were necessary to finance the trip. Sheila returned to Glentex, a small scarf manufacturer, and I got a fulltime job at Escuela Hispana Montessori, a head start program in the "far east" on Avenue D and Houston St, in the Lillian Wald Housing projects.

Escuela Hispana was unique, because it was the first Spanish Montessori Head Start program in the country, and although designed for the poor and working class, it also attracted middle and upper middle-class families. It became a meeting ground for children and families of very different backgrounds.

Similar to Two Bridges, Escuela was a rich, varied tapestry of people with similar political views, needs and aspirations. Many of the parents and employees found it to be a milky way for personal growth. This diverse environment reflected a microcosm of NYC, enriching both the children and their parents.

Sheila often visited me at work, and she became so enamored of the children and the dynamics of the program that it changed her life goals and set her on a path to become an educator. Each June, the oldest children, who were turning five, would have a graduation, with pink or blue caps and gowns, to reflect female or male student.

When I asked, "Why such a formal ceremony at this age", Judy, the director, stated, "Because for many children, this will be the last graduation they will experience". For the first time, I felt that I found a role and a place where a profound service was rendered, a service I was proud to support. My experience there became the foundation for what later became my career.

Each day, I pedaled my bike to work, and then came home to make dinner with Sheila. We joined a meat co-op on Little West 12th Street, and monthly we would lug home ten to twenty pounds of meat: skirt steaks, porterhouse, T-bone, brisket, etc.

To me, it felt like a "homage" to my father, because I would slice most of the fat off the meat, cut it into meal portions, and wrap it for freezing, just as I imagined my father once did as a butcher. Food, like lovemaking, was not only important to me, but became central to our relationship. We experimented with recipes from various regions of the world, baked bread, made desserts and salad dressings.

As we gained confidence in our cooking we changed recipe ingredients and spicing to fit our vision and palate. The daily activity of cooking filled us, nurtured our spirits and brought us closer together. Even then, preparing and sharing food with friends, drinking wine and listening to music were vital to our relationship and communication with others.

As we became closer, Sheila and I became more aware of how we differed from one another, and, at times, how difficult that was. We each dealt with challenges differently. Sheila would take a longer time than I could tolerate to respond or try to solve the rift between us.

I was so threatened that I needed to reduce the emotional distance between us immediately. The fact that Sheila needed space to be alone, threatened my very core. To me, it meant that she was withdrawing her love, as my mother did when she was angry. I feared that Sheila was leaving me or becoming involved with someone else, when in fact she simply needed her own space.

There was a feeling deep inside of me that soothed my fears and gave me confidence that Sheila was right for me, although love had not yet risen to the surface. In contrast, I displayed bursts of anger latent since childhood. This deep-felt rage could be triggered in a nanosecond and like a charge of electricity could slice a person in half. It was the only emotion I truly owned.

It would take another five years before my love for Sheila crystalized. I was not quick to acknowledge love, to go out on a limb, to trust, or to commit. My experience told me to guard my emotions and not share completely, because life is ephemeral, and loss lurks in the shadows.

Not long after one of these blow-ups, I learned that my parents, aunts and uncles, were returning to live in Holland to establish the necessary residency required before they could collect WWII reparation funds. As much as I had distanced myself from my parents, I always expected them to be there if I needed them. To hear that they needed to exit my world, reopened the old wounds of abandonment that I felt as a young child, when I was ripped away from Moeder and Vader.

Weeks thereafter at JFK Airport, Marja and I consoled one another, as we bid our parents goodbye. Although we didn't know it at the time, this sudden rupture would be fortuitous, for both of us.

Until then, my emotional "umbilical" connectedness had never been tested or severed. Because I feared abandonment, I unconsciously wove layers of emotions and developed a symbiosis with them. Now, I felt abandoned, hurt and angry. I pouted and distanced myself further by rarely calling or writing them.

In retrospect, the sudden rupture from my parents, accelerated my struggle to become whole and independent. At the time, the separation was even worse for cousin Marion, who found herself caring for her younger siblings, when her parents returned to Holland. Although twenty-one and married to Jimmy for three years, she gave emotional and physical sustenance to her teen-aged brother and sister Rosie, while still growing up herself.

22

Sheila and I were building a strong bond, and looked forward to our pending trip in the fall of 1971. We had now worked fulltime for a year and had squirreled away five thousand dollars, a fortune at that time. Icelandic Airlines had a special fare of $168 for an open round-trip ticket that allowed up to a year of use between leaving and returning to the States.

I had mixed feelings about leaving my job, but the sirens of travel were beckoning. After we found someone to sub-let our apartment and care for our cats, we planned our itinerary and bought camping equipment. To keep costs low we intended to hitchhike everywhere and camp wherever possible. A New York Times travel article about Agadir, Morocco and its three hundred days of sun, became our destination and set us in motion.

Reykjavik Airport was neon lit, so bright that we were forced to wear sun glasses as we walked through the terminals and stores on our way to the plane that would take us to Luxembourg. When we arrived in Luxembourg, the streets were wet from the morning rains and here and there shopkeepers were opening their stores, cleaning sidewalks and drinking their morning coffee. After exploring the city for a few hours, we found a small hotel, promptly took a nap and then shared a wonderful meal of *filet mignon*, roasted potatoes *au jus*, green salad and red wine.

The following morning, we headed to the nearest highway that would take us north through Belgium into Holland to visit my parents, who resided ironically on Onderduikersstraat (Underground Street) in Groningen. These were the days when hitchhiking was safe and popular and drivers of all ages felt comfortable, if not eager, to pick up strangers. Post-war western Europe was bustling with optimism and commerce. Everything was seen through rose-colored glasses. The dollar was strong and made travelling that much more palatable for Americans.

It took us a full day to reach Groningen and we arrived after dinner. My mother reheated the *kipragout* (chicken fricasse) they had eaten earlier that evening. Made with a hint of mace, mommy scooped the chicken over the steamy potatoes and then poured some of the buttery chicken gravy over it. To say this was sublime would not capture the satisfaction and bliss I experienced as I stuffed myself full, like a suckling pig ready to be put on the spit. Although quite bloated, I slept deeply that night, happy to be in my parents' home.

Once again, I was with my parents, but unlike our reunion after the war, this time it was on my own terms. I was surprised that I had missed them, and I savored the sensations of nurturing and security that I felt with them, perhaps for the first time.

My parents' apartment was near a municipal park that had a small petting zoo and a large field where kids played soccer. Their first-floor space, filled with sunlight, was warm and inviting and they had a small grassy backyard surrounded by bushes and flowers.

The apartment was within strolling distance of downtown Groningen, and I remembered the various places I walked to as a child: the Grote Markt, the old Stadhuis, Martini Kerk and the public square. All this, and whiffs of tobacco from the Niemeyer factory, enveloped me in nostalgia, with sweet and painful tears. The moist, cold December air clung to our bones, and we were eager for a warmer, sunnier climate.

We decided to go south, through Holland, Belgium, France, and Spain, to Morocco. Our plan to travel for eight months, possibly a year meant that we needed to spend more time in countries where the cost of living was lower.

The following day, Sheila and I bought bicycles. We planned to pedal to Amsterdam, a mere hundred and ten miles from Groningen. The bikes, were the Clydesdales of the bicycle world. They were big and clunky, with only three speeds and hard leather seats. Brown canvas saddle bags, that rested on the rear of the bicycles and held our gear, were a practical alternative to our backpacks.

We decided to test out the bikes later that day by taking a ride to the nearby city of Assen, my mother's birthplace.

Somehow, Sheila and I got separated on our way back to Groningen. Unable to find her, I continued towards Groningen, hoping that she would do the same.

Still missing an hour later, I became increasingly anxious. When she finally arrived, rather than greeting her with a warm embrace and a face full of concern, my anxiety bubbled over into anger, and I raged at her. This subterranean anger, like a riverbed filled by a rush of mountain rains, would divide us from time to time and remained a major obstacle in our relationship for many years.

I didn't realize at the time, but much to my chagrin, I mimicked my father's emotional response to situations that caused him fear or concern. Whenever my father had an important, civil discussion with my mother, he would almost immediately change into a raving lunatic. Like an out-of-control train, he bellowed on, and this could go on for days. It struck fear into all of us, including him. I don't know if these instances were caused by his traumatic experiences in the war, but they certainly added fuel to his anger.

A few days later, we pedaled away, looking back to see my parents waving goodbye. About thirty miles into our adventure, the pedaling became harder and our optimism for reaching Amsterdam on bike faded. We arrived in Zwolle late in the afternoon and stiffly walked around like cowboys after a month on the range. We promptly sold the bikes and going forward, we would wear our thumbs out rather than our limbs. Relieved to reach Amsterdam by noon, we immediately checked into a small neighborhood hotel and stayed in bed for the rest of the day and night.

The Dutch breakfast is something to behold. The next morning, sitting at a table covered with a table cloth that looked more like a thin rug, we had a typical Dutch breakfast. The strong coffee with "koffiemelk", the Dutch version of evaporated milk, was followed by soft boiled eggs and hearty farmers bread slathered with butter. Soon thereafter a chunk of young gouda cheese, a variety of jams, ham, sausage, and oranges appeared. The breakfast was not only sumptuous but dazzled my senses. By the time we continued on to Maastricht, we decided to sell the canvas bags as well, finding them to be unnecessary weight.

Before Maastricht we stopped in Breda, and stayed overnight with my cousin Harold, the economist, and his wife Marion. They were gracious and warm, even though Sheila and I came unannounced. Still, the awkwardness hung like a heavy cloud, and we left early the following day. Although we should have known better, we were living an alternative lifestyle where dropping in was considered normal. On the other hand, Harold who lived a more traditional life, must have thought we were rude and immature.

The southern city of Maastricht, formerly an outpost of the Roman empire, is the central hub of the province of Limburg and is part of an area uncharacteristically hilly. We were captivated by the city, its airiness and culture, but especially its hand-cut pommes frites served with thick *mayonaise*. Each day we found ourselves at a pommes frites stand to get our daily fix and reluctantly left Maastricht and our pommes frites several days later.

We made our way to Paris, but had decided before we began our trip to focus our attention on people and witnessing daily life in small towns, villages and hamlets, rather than spending time in large cities. Perversely, the many places we moved to when I was a child and created so many problems in my life, paradoxically made me a professional traveler. I was quite comfortable on the open road.

Travelling south, toward Avignon we hitched a ride with a driver who seemed like a race car fanatic. He wore racing gloves and at one point passed a car that was passing another car on a one lane highway. Fortunately, his low-to-the ground Citroen safely sped by, and fifteen minutes later we wobbled out of the car, glad to be on firm ground.

We decided to visit the Pont du Gard, the highest Roman aqueduct, overlooking the Gardon River. We were part of a large gaggle of tourists being guided across the former water delivery route. The valley below, the lush green trees on the banks of the river, the strong cool breezes and the sheer height of the aqueduct made one feel insignificant and yet part of the scheme of life.

It also was terrifying for me, not because I was afraid of heights, but because Sheila suddenly moved close to one edge. I felt weights encumbering my calf muscles, shinbones and ankles, and to her surprise, I dashed over and pulled her back. I worried that she might lose her balance, but her fearlessness threatened me even more.

I was becoming more and more attached to Sheila, and our

relationship had become deeper than before. Though my feelings were all tangled up, I had a clear, if not visceral reaction when she moved toward the edge, which was one of fear and loss.

After Avignon, we stayed in the southern city of Perpignan, near the Mediterranean Sea and the Pyrenees Mountains. The air felt almost salty, and although it was December, there was a suggestion of spring, and small purple flowers that grew near the rocky base of the Pyrenees were in bloom.

Two days before New Year, my sister Marja visited us in this hilly medieval city and we celebrated New Year's together. This was still a time when I could do no wrong in Marja's eyes and I was still living the dream. Armed with baguettes, cheese and wine, we took long walks to Canet Plage, picnicking in olive groves, as we made our way to the beach.

A few days after New Year's, we bid Marja farewell, as she took the long train ride north back to Groningen. We, on the other hand, decided to enter Spain over the Pyrenees, but much to our surprise, found a winter wonderland, and the road impassable. At the summit, there was an endless vision of deep snow, with no tire markings and I decided to baptize the virgin snow with my urine. We turned around and drove down the narrow mountain road and made our way to Barcelona along the sun-drenched coast.

This Catalan capital port city was teeming with life. The airiness and liveliness of this grand city, with its independently minded, proud people, was immediately apparent. Franco's boot of authority, which was visible in the form of the civil guard, national guard and secret police, did not interrupt the rhythm of the city. As we travelled further south to more conservative areas, hitchhiking became almost impossible and we began to rely more and more on public transportation.

It was on a bus trip to Granada that we traveled through Andalusia, the rich, agrarian valley, that lay in stark contrast to the drab brown homes that were carved out of the sides of the mountain. Although the people on the bus were chatting amiably with one another, Sheila and I were acutely aware that when the bus hugged a curve, one of its back tires was usually hanging in space. We took a deep breath of relief when the bus driver yelled out, "Granada", and we spilled out onto the dusty road.

Arriving without cash, we picked the most expensive hotel, knowing we could exchange money when we paid our bill. That night we ate in the hotel dining room, where the twenty-foot high ceiling was adorned with frescos and sparkling chandeliers.

We had been on the road camping for over a month, and this was the first of several instances of pure indulgence in contrast to our daily austerity. Two days later, when the banks opened, we paid our bill in cash. In my heart, I was still a hidden child. I knew that credit cards would identify me, put me on the map as it were, and were a form of registering as my parents had done many years before. I was not ready to do that in 1972.

Continuing south, it was in Malaga that I heard wafts of Arabic music, beckoning me to go further south into North Africa. I was overwhelmed with feelings of intrigue and nostalgia, remembering my experiences in Israel almost twenty years before. We were happy to leave Malaga the following day, not only because our hotel mattress felt like we were sleeping in a gulley, but the city itself was in complete decline and tourists were ripe for fleecing, like flies on raw meat.

Torremolinos, our next resting place, was less than half an hour further along the Costa del Sol but felt like a different world. If it weren't for the Spanish architecture and language, it might have passed for a sleepy coastal New England village, with a British Penguin bookstore, a few restaurants, some hotels and clusters of cottages that dotted the hillside like white mushrooms.

A British tourist hub, it was sparsely populated in January. We decided to stay in a cottage colony called, "Mi Paradiso", owned by two British men, one of whom had previously lived in India. When we were shown the cottage by the manager / cleaning woman, she made a point of telling us that if anything was missing or broken we would have to pay for it. We thought it was comical. The cottage contained the bare necessities and the only decoration was a cheap plaster bust of the Madonna.

Each day we meandered to the beach area of the town to have our morning coffee and tea, read the Herald Tribune, and peruse the bookstore and nearby shops. It was on one of those occasions that I found a used copy of Thomas Mann's *Young Joseph*, the second volume of a four-volume set, of *Joseph and His Brothers*.

I had always been an avid Mann reader, with *The Magic Mountain* being my favorite book, specifically because of Mann's description of the concept of time, and his portrayal of the Dionysian, Dutch character, Mijnheer Peeperkorn. Young Joseph, the narcissistic boy, whose young mother, Rachel, was Jacob's favorite wife, fled clandestinely to Egypt to escape his stepbrothers. His experiences melded into a bridge that I moved across, reliving my own hidden past and moving to places unknown in the present.

Young Joseph opened a window in my mind conjuring images of my childhood in Israel filled with olives and figs, goats and sheep, scraggly hills and lush river beds, a landscape typifying the Middle East and Morocco. The book became my traveling bible. Nibbling at it slowly, I hoped that it would last indefinitely.

A few days later, after returning from a walk, Sheila noticed that the plaster Madonna was missing from our room. We looked everywhere and much to our chagrin, surmised that that it was a scam to make us pay for the missing bust. We were angry and knew that it would be the manager's word against ours and that she had the upper hand.

Early the next morning, before daylight we absconded with our gear, and in retribution, took a blanket and a special "sock / filter" for coffee making. Anxiously, we made our way to the main road, fearing that we would be followed, and were fortunate to get a ride right away. Twenty minutes later, we passed through the bustling tourist town of Marbella, on our way to the port at Algeciras.

23

The ferry ride across the Mediterranean was surprisingly swift and uneventful, except for the myriad of colors, textures and designs of kaftans, djellabas, African skullcaps, and leather rubber-soled sandals worn by many of the passengers.

When we landed at the port of Tangiers, Sheila and I, unlike the many who lived there or came sightseeing and shopping for the day, headed straight for the highway. We had heard enough about this port city and knew that tourists were easy prey.

It was noon, a light warm rain greeted us as we fervently stuck our thumbs out in hopes of reaching Casablanca or Ad-Dar al-Bayda by nightfall. A man dressed in western attire and an African skullcap and travelling with his teenage son, picked us up and immediately wanted to practice his English.

Since the drive took almost four hours, the discussion, mostly one-sided, shifted from one question to another: "Where are you from?", "Where are you going?", "My name is Yousif, what is yours?", "I worked in Holland last year", "Do you like our country?". Our driver, who was on his way to Essaouira, dropped us off at the outskirts of Casablanca.

It seemed like we walked for several miles before we found a small inn to stay overnight. The exotic city of Casablanca that Humphrey Bogart and Ingrid Bergman painted so vividly in 1942 had been eclipsed and transformed into a city where the trees were dwarfed by white and grey modern concrete buildings. The generic western quality of the city surprised and disappointed us.

We left as early as possible the following morning to continue our journey, consciously avoiding popular tourist areas, and went inland towards Marrakech. We reached the outskirts of Marrakech, the faded, red-walled city and, treating ourselves to a ride in a horse and carriage, we passed by La Mamounia, the pink palace-like historic hotel.

Giant-sized doormen dressed in white stood frozen at the doorway entrance and magical gardens surrounded the hotel, a botanical bacchanal that contrasted sharply with our camp grounds, where the almost barren mud-baked terrain looked more like a municipal parking lot. The drab campsite, like a blank canvas, was infused with an array of colors and shapes of tents, camping gear, dogs, music, children, the smell of cooked food, vapors of hashish and marijuana, and a variety of automobiles.

Marrakech, at the foot hills of the Atlas Mountains, was and is a center for trade and culture for all of Africa and had been for hundreds of years. This Berber city was still a sleepy city and not yet the mecca for tourism that it later became.

That said, through word of mouth, it was already a capital of sorts for long-haired, counter-culture hippies from across the western world. Everyone was on their way somewhere: home, India, Sicily, or Greece. Some people, especially many of the Australians we met had been travelling for years. Like me, many people were searching for something, personal identity, home or spirituality.

We made daily excursions to the old city or medina and the square called Jamaa el Fna, the Assembly of the Dead, and followed the many snake-like alleyways and streets making up the Souk, or marketplace. Jamaa was a magnet for all kinds of entertainment and commerce: water men with silver cups hanging around their necks, snake charmers, story tellers, food sellers hawking fresh-baked round barley bread, spices and fruit vendors. Many young boys swarmed like honey bees, moving from one tourist to another, willing to take pictures for any currency or eager to trade Moroccan pieces of clothing or trinkets for highly coveted denim jeans.

By evening, Jamaa would transform into a huge outdoor picnic ground, with stall after stall offering a variety of freshly made street food served at long tables and benches. Crowds would gather around one performer or another and this was also a ripe time for pickpockets to ply their trade.

Our NYC street smarts kept us extra vigilant and it made me reflect on another time, when I was so needy that I stole from others. It was the large daytime Souk with its labyrinth of streets, that dazzled us most. These narrow paths, covered overhead with wooden slats to keep out the noon day sun, held the mystery of a culture that bridged a thousand years into the past. The vibrant colors, endless displays of redundant merchandise: tea glasses, Berber rugs, ceramics, silver jewelry, spices, nylon stockings, fresh figs, dates and roasted nuts were a kaleidoscope of visual poetry. Near the end of each pathway, the shops and stalls were replaced by blacksmiths, auto repair stalls, holding pens for livestock and homes.

The competition was intense amongst the merchants and each one called out hoping to convince us that their merchandise was the best. In contrast to Sheila, who was very uncomfortable bargaining, I became a master negotiator, and sometimes I would take days to bargain for a single item. The pleasure that I derived from this custom was not only the ability to get a reasonable price but the communication it opened between myself and the merchant.

In my quest for finding my voice and space in this universe, I always sought fulfillment through communication and community. In the process of bargaining I learned that the merchant had an unwed daughter, a toothache, or that he fought for the French at Dien Bien Phu. Bargaining was a way of learning about one another and recognizing the merchant as someone with a history, a life, and feelings. Sometimes we were even invited to lunch and continued to bargain after our meal. When the negotiations ended, I walked away smiling, knowing that I still paid too much but reveled in the experience.

I felt that we were not just passing through this country like tourists, but were invested in the culture and adjusting to their sense of time. When time slows down for me, I become unaware of it, and only then do I feel unburdened, free and at peace. I am sure that having Sheila as a companion on this trip, sharing more and more with her, enriched and sustained me as well.

Although we could easily have spent weeks in Marrakech, we were eager to make our way to the southern coastal city of Agadir. Instead of hitchhiking west to Essaouira, we elected to go the longer and more difficult route through the Atlas mountain range. The Moroccan driver regaled us with stories of his youth, as we nervously drove through the snow leaving fresh tire marks in our wake. The driver wanted to reach Tizi-n-Test pass before dark, not only because his aunt lived in the area, but the road was especially treacherous at night.

Though we reached the "pass" well before darkness fell, I had difficulty sleeping that night and did not look forward to driving further along this narrow winding road the following morning. The distance was about a hundred and forty miles, and it took us close to eight hours to navigate the steep, narrow road. The trip, though beautiful, could not pass fast enough. Late in the afternoon, elated and exhausted, we reached the well-preserved, amber-colored ramparts of Taroudant, a smaller version of Marrakech, where we stayed for the night.

After a short ride—at least in contrast to the day before—the jeep made its way to the Atlantic coast and Agadir.

The city had suffered a devastating earthquake eleven years earlier and was completely rebuilt. Except for the manicured orange trees and a modern luxury hotel, what we saw were rows of concrete sidewalks connecting to drab looking homes, one less appealing than the next. Even worse was the eerie silence that we witnessed, since many of the homes had just been developed and were not yet occupied. Fortunately, we had already revised our plans, since we heard that there was a colony of long-haired folks living on a beach in a nearby fishing village called Taghazout.

It was as though we had landed in an alien universe when we arrived at Taghazout (Tarazoot). Except for a cafe in the distance, a streak of banana trees, and a camp ground full of trailers on a hill, the beach was littered with small geodesic dome-like huts. As we made our way across the sand, we noticed on closer inspection that these "domes" were made from young bamboo saplings bent into overlapping arcs. The saplings were tied to one another and covered with thick translucent plastic sheets that were pegged down on all sides. These "dachas", large enough to comfortably fit four or more people, were hot houses during the daytime, whenever the sun was out, which was every day.

We paid fifteen dollars or the equivalent in dirhams for one of these condos. Our Buckminster Fuller "dome" house, well-built and cleverly designed, had straw matting inside, which allowed the sand to filter through. Adjacent to our dome was a large circular cooking pit about two feet deep and four feet in diameter.

It housed a small metal stand on top of which sat a fired clay tagine.

Within the pit, also carved out of sand, was a sturdy, molded bench where we could comfortably sit while we cooked. Next to the cooking pit our "dome" architect had created a primitive, fully functioning refrigeration unit. Dug deep into the sand, the narrow hole had two large flat overlapping stones that lined the bottom. Because the hole was so deep, the cool, moist sand kept margarine, eggs, oranges and other perishables preserved for five to six days.

Cooking together and sharing meals was a blessing. Sheila and I loved to create endless combinations of vegetables that we seasoned with cumin and other Moroccan spices bought at the local souk. All this went into the tagine bottom to steam. Once the vegetables were softened and their juices appeared, we added couscous and cracked eggs over the mixture and covered it with the conical-shaped lid.

The results were so sumptuous that, except for varying the protein, we had versions of the same dish most evenings and never tired of it. We were literally less than fifty feet from the Atlantic Ocean's waves, and at dusk we sat along the edge of a dune with other campers, like seagulls to watch the orange sun fold into the blue water. Like a giant parachute sending rays of light in all directions, the sun slowly faded into the evening mist.

The five-acre beach front was dotted with at least forty plastic domes and a few tents sandwiched in between. On the hillside there were trailers mostly owned by German expats, who no doubt had been in Morocco during World War II, and returned after retirement. Many of the dome community, both male and female, sunned themselves in the nude. We didn't have any problem with nude bathing, but in such a conservative culture, where women young and old, wore layers of clothing, we found it arrogant and offensive.

As an Islamic country, it was best for western women to be with a male companion, since they were viewed as whores. Even if they were completely covered, they were still ogled like a piece of ripe fruit ready for the tasting.

Once a week we bathed and washed our clothes at the public baths in Agadir and treated ourselves to sandwiches from Charlie's Deli. Charlie's had been discovered by some of the beach hippies and word spread about his fresh, gargantuan sandwiches. Warm baked rounds of flat bread filled with sardines, tuna or chunks of cheese, spices and fresh vegetables, were a feast for our senses and this celebration became a weekly ritual.

After Charlie's we made our way to the farmer's souk, where we bought our weekly provisions. Every item was a negotiation and I delighted in the process. Our filet bags brimming with food, we hitched back to our home on the beach.

With the exception of our weekly trip to Agadir, we were content to stay on the beach, where we cooked, read, got high, swam, sunbathed, napped, and foraged for dry eucalyptus leaves, twigs and branches for the cooking fire. Every morning at daylight, we diligently guarded our plastic home until a herd of hungry goats and one old, scarred camel passed by.

We once soberly witnessed a condo swallowed almost whole by these ravenous, rambunctious goats, as our neighbor rushed back to save his bamboo skeleton. An old man on his donkey finally led them away to the lush grasses on the edge of a riverbed to graze.

Each day flowed into another. I practiced my karate every morning and the local people at the café called me, "Mustache Karate". I felt on top of the moment. Ever aware of time and its restrictions, I had never experienced living outside the frame of time.

Shackled by responsibilities and loss for so many years, this new freedom was exhilarating, and I savored its sweetness like a fine Moroccan pastry. More than six weeks had passed since we purchased our condo, routines had been set, friendships were made, and a small brown puppy entered our lives.

Dogs in Morocco are the lowest creatures on the totem pole of recognition and respect. As a result, they are mean, haggard and scrawny. In order to gain an extra morsel of food they are extremely protective of their turf. In fact, on one occasion, Sheila and I, and our friend Richard, needed to slowly back away from a group of semi-feral dogs. Fur raised, teeth clenched they would have made mince-meat of us, had we turned and ran. Sheila, who had been attacked by a German shepherd as a child, was deathly afraid of dogs. She froze in fear and, unable to move, Richard and I slowly dragged her away.

In contrast, Gopher, the short-haired brown puppy that was four to six months old, walked right into Sheila's heart. We agreed to care for him while our neighbor travelled.

A week later our neighbor returned, but by that time we had bonded with the pooch and he with us. We convinced our fellow traveler that Gopher was meant to stay with us and, to our surprise, he agreed. Gopher would follow Sheila wherever she went. He was her companion and in some ways gave her recognition in a country where women were devoid of visibility.

Whereas most days flowed into one another, creating continuity and a sense of peacefulness, there were still nights when recurring dreams would torment me. Since we left Mi Paradiso I would have periodic nightmares that thematically related to being "found out".

That anxiety had permeated my DNA since WWII and manifested itself in different ways. I feared I would be found incompetent, perceived as less than what the universe expected and someone who makes mistakes. Mistakes in my family's history spelled danger or possibly death.

In those moments I felt helpless, as though in a police line-up, being peered at by witnesses, who were encouraged to match me to all the unsolved cases on the station house blotter. As a result, there were nights I was so anxious that I refused to go to sleep, for fear that these dreams would surface again. I don't know if these dreams had to do with my early beginnings or a lack of trust that the good times would last, but again it reminded me that life is ever changing.

It was the beginning of spring, and with the start of the rainy season a gust of new travelers, including Robin, the Albanian arrived. He and his small clan travelled annually between western Europe and Morocco, selling and buying a variety of goods. He bought *hashish* (kief) and Moroccan rugs to sell in Germany and other European countries.

Essentially, he would buy anything from which he could make a profit. He lived in a lavish tent with his entourage. The tent, made of large heavy canvas, was held aloft by thick, six-foot poles and secured on each side by sturdy wooden pegs. Inside, the floor was covered with many multi-colored carpets, several mattresses, assorted pillows, and a low table. Unlike the smaller tents and plastic domes, his tent was on higher, hardened ground, and shaded by two enormous Atlas cedar trees.

Robin's chiseled features, high cheekbones, short-cropped hair, manicured beard, lean, muscular body, and magical "herbs", gave him a cult-like stature on the beach, and he used it to his advantage. This earlier version of a "Charles Manson" profile worked well for him, and he had many followers who idolized him. I, on the other hand, could never tolerate such blind submissiveness towards humans or gods, and as much as I wished to be liked and respected, and to reciprocate in kind, any form of idolatry felt totally threatening. Robin, the narcissist, realized that I would never be at his beck and call, so he and I achieved the next best thing, which was a détente.

A week later, Robin invited Sheila and I to travel south to the city of Goulimine, known as the gateway to the Sahara. This adventure sounded just right, and once arrangements were made for Gopher and our plastic abode, we jumped into his old Land Rover, that was large enough to fit ten people plus gear. Four hours later we reached Goulimine, a small, dusty frontier-like city, where the only bank transformed into a fruit and vegetable market four times a week and the traffic of camel, horses, goats, people and vehicles, seemed to never end.

As we entered the town, teenage boys approached the Land Rover offering piping hot *shay nana* (mint tea) and decorative metal platters filled with slices of small blood-red oranges. It was Friday noon and people were streaming out of the mosque, while others were shopping. The two groups blended, creating a frenetic burst of energy and excitement that filled the medina. After we bought some supplies, we drove for about ten minutes from Goulimine to Abbainou, where we camped for three days. The hot springs at this tiny oasis attracted many travelers, and its proximity to Goulimine made it an ideal camping area.

Sheila and I noticed the seediness of the place immediately. As we started to pitch our small tent, two Moroccan women dressed in long sleeved black kaftans and headscarves, made inviting sexual gestures towards me to buy their services. Later, after we set up our campsite, we took a short walk and found two naked female travelers floating on their backs in the muddy waters of one of the hot springs.

Their hair was dyed a wine-red color and their hands and feet were decorated with blue henna. A gaggle of Moroccan men stood nearby, gawking and smiling, while the European women, oblivious to local culture and the men, continued to romp in the murky waters. In the evening, tired of reading by our Coleman lamp, I put on my rough woolen djellaba and, as though in a trance, I stared endlessly at the desert night sky illuminated by countless flickering stars, while Sheila slept peacefully in our narrow mountain tent.

The following evening, we went to what we thought was a dinner party in Robin's tent, and were surprised to find many people, mostly strangers, inside and outside the big tent. Two goats on separate spits were being slowly turned over an open fire, the juices dripping into pans beneath. The smell of smoke, sweet meat, lemon and mint enveloped our nostrils, awakened our appetites and made our eyes tear.

We opened the flap of the tent to find a group of people sitting quietly and feeding each other spoons of what looked like molasses. The syrupy dark substance in the bowl was called *Mahjoun*, a Berber jam, made from honey and various nuts mixed with dates, figs, butter, rose water, and—most importantly—hashish. The thick syrup, when eaten directly, is a hallucinogen, and although I enjoyed it, Sheila had a negative reaction, compelling her to return to our tent. Feeling unable to breathe she sat inside the tent and her head sticking outside, gasping for air throughout the night. People moved in and out of Robin's tent all night, but it didn't matter to me. I remained horizontal. It felt as though I was in a Victorian opium den.

The desert sun is merciless, and escape into any shade is a must. Thus, when Robin decided to go further south and west towards the Atlantic coast and the city of Tan-Tan we were happy to oblige. Off the barely visible road, two men dressed in flowing light-blue robes, blue scarves covering everything except nose and eyes, raced each other on camels, as we neared the port city.

Tan-Tan seemed more like a Las Vegas strip than a Moroccan medina, with its glitzy neon lights and seediness. There was a sense of lawlessness in this duty-free port, where one could find American cigarettes, local leather products and silver jewelry, side-by-side with small electrical appliances and guns.

While Robin was busy negotiating a deal, we walked on the beach and gathered an array of unusually beautiful, smooth, multi-colored stones. Collectively, they must have weighed twenty or more pounds, but we were determined to bring them back to the US.

Later the same day, after Robin had loaded many cartons of cigarettes onto the Land Rover, we drove off into the desert. Five minutes into the drive, we could see several vehicles following distantly behind us and heard what sounded like fire crackers, but were actually rifle shots aimed in our direction.

Robin floored the Land Rover, as all of us—frightened and bewildered—clutched tightly to the metal edge of our seats. This surreal event felt surprisingly familiar and reminded me of childhood experiences when life was ruptured and I was afraid, helpless and numb. Robin never told us why we were shot at. We surmised that they were police, or merchants, or Polisario (a West Saharan rebel group), who Robin might have cheated or robbed.

A day later, we returned to Taghazout to find an ecstatic puppy and our poor man's Buckminster Fuller geodesic home still intact. Neighbors told us that it had rained for days and that many travelers had left. Their domes and disintegrating bamboo frames, like skeletal remains, gave the community an air of transience and decay.

For Sheila the rain meant she could stay inside to read and draw without the intense, oppressive sun on top of her. But, on this morning we were disturbed by a roar that became louder and louder, followed by the screams of various people and the scurrying of feet outside our dome. As we stepped out, we could see that the dry riverbed had been overrun by the rush of mountain water, mud, rocks and branches.

A donkey, left by a shepherd to graze in the dry riverbed while he took his goats a few kilometers away, was caught up in the gush of floating debris and was being carried out to sea. Not struggling at all, it was clearly in shock. A group of people stood around yelling, one was taking photos, when I and a few others plunged in where the sea and river met. Greeted by chest high water, we pulled the donkey back ashore. The donkey lay there on its side, struggling to breathe, bewildered, glassy eyed and trembling. We covered him with a blanket, and rubbed his side briskly.

Suddenly, like Lazarus rising from the dead, he stood up, belched and lots of water rushed from his mouth. The small crowd cheered. Soon the shepherd returned, thanked the rescuers, and took the animal with the rest of his flock, and slowly moved on. I felt heroic, but more importantly, I acted spontaneously and took control. Normally, I am vigilant, censoring my actions, but at that moment I was no longer hidden. I acted with resolve—without fear of the consequences—and had helped save a life. It was amazing, but not completely surprising to see how life could be safe and serene one moment and dangerous and turbulent the next.

The rain clouds and sun dueled for attention as March ended. Sheila and I decided not to renew our visas, dictating that we needed to leave Morocco soon. However, that decision was accelerated by the disintegration of sanitary conditions, people getting ill, and by a horrific event.

We heard that a four-year-old boy had been kidnapped. A young Danish family, who had recently arrived, informed the local police that he was missing and placed flyers everywhere. They combed the area, without result, while rumors suggested that Robin had something to do with it.

Whether true or not, we reluctantly gave our puppy back to our neighbor, and hit the road. Leaving Gopher behind was hard for me, but I was now older and I was not alone. The comfort Sheila provided made it less difficult. This time we decided to travel along the coast, and by early afternoon we had reached Essaouira.

The blue and white port city, prized for its seafood and ice cream, its Portuguese fortresses, French and Moorish architecture, was a wonderful relief from the disturbing events in our beach community. We stayed at a campsite and proceeded back to Marrakech the next day.

It was late afternoon when we arrived in Marrakech. Passing food stalls along the way to the campsite, the air was filled with the vapors of food being prepared for the evening meal. I salivated as I thought of a tagine filled with garlic, onions, cauliflower, prunes, almonds and lamb shank.

The campsite, though familiar and inviting, seemed less exotic and there were fewer fellow travelers. We slept soundly but were awakened by nightmares. Surprisingly, both of our dreams dealt with death and loss. Sheila dreamt that her cat, Millicent, was stabbed, and I dreamt that Gopher kept running towards me, but something was holding him back. Sadly, days later, we heard that our puppy, Gopher had been stabbed by our unbalanced neighbor in Taghazout because he no longer wanted to be burdened with his care. I envisioned that he didn't think twice before killing him, after all he was only a dog, and the thought made me shudder.

Our sadness seemed to weigh as much as the Tan-Tan beach stones in our knapsacks. Glad to leave the following morning for Ceuta, the Spanish passageway to Spain and Europe, we were intent on returning to Holland, or "Mama Land", as we now called it, as soon as possible. Nothing could be more soothing than to be cared for as only parents can, to be served warm food, to sleep between clean sheets, and to feel rejuvenated. Maybe I was beginning the healing process.

We arrived in Madrid a week later. There, we gladly lightened our backpacks by shipping the stones and several other items home to the States. The following day we traveled west to Burgos and took the night train to Paris. Refreshed from a good night's sleep and less burdened by the weight of our packs, our spirits rose. We departed from Gare du Nord, ready to make our way to "Mama Land".

24

It was more than six months since we had been in Holland and, in contrast to October, daylight now persisted until nine pm. The dampness had disappeared and there were fresh strawberries and tulips in every market stall. The six months not only reflected the differences of seasons, but highlighted the changes in our relationship.

The intensity of travel can hide, delay or crystallize change, and in our case, it was the latter. We were more aware of each other's needs, and our trust for one another had grown. We felt like partners, lovers and best friends, holding each other's heart. Psychologically, I was committed to Sheila, liked and respected her, but my feelings of love and empathy were still blocked.

My parents were blocked in a different way. Their world was static. They were either incapable or unwilling to forge new friendships and their social life revolved solely around family. With Oom Jules and Tante Emmy, they talked of moving closer to the rest of the family in Amsterdam so that they could replicate the "Friday nights" they had experienced with great satisfaction in America.

They were considering a move to a new apartment complex on the outskirts of Amsterdam, called *Bijlmermeer*. Though I questioned the move at that time, in retrospect it made perfect sense for them.

Feeling rejuvenated, after our stay in Groningen, we decided to travel to Denmark and Sweden. Our objective was to visit Roy, a friend who fled the US to avoid the Draft. Camped in a lush, woodsy, vest-pocket park in a suburb just outside of Copenhagen, we pitched our little tent, made sumptuous meals, and played rousing games of Gin Rummy.

Each morning, while we made our coffee and prepared breakfast, local people strolled by, accompanied by their dogs or children. Some would greet us, astonished to see campers there, while others were oblivious to our presence in their neighborhood park.

A few days later, we reached Stockholm and walked to the University. Roy lived on the campus of the University of Stockholm, where he took a few courses. The Swedish social welfare state was at the European forefront in accommodating political asylum seekers from all over the world. Roy was the only person that we knew who could do the Sunday Times crossword puzzle in ink. He was confident of his puzzle skills, as he was about most things that he did, including leaving the US because of deep-held convictions about the Vietnam War.

The city of Stockholm was a composite of many islands, bridges, cobblestone streets and diverse architecture. Bright sunlight belied the sobering darkness of long lines of Swedes clutching their shopping bags, waiting for the *Systembolaget*, the state liquor stores, to open. Finnish people seemed to perform all the necessary but least desirable work, and the Swedes viewed them as inferior and treated them with contempt. Roy ultimately moved to Lapland, married a Finnish woman, and still lives there today.

After a week in Stockholm we decided to return to Holland. Every travel experience after Morocco was anti-climactic, and we were ready to go back to the States—to go home. It was early August, and it was time to leave "Mama Land" and return to the US and continue our lives.

The nine plus months of travel transformed our relationship and melded us into a serious couple. It created a foundation, where there was none before, and as a result, the rhythm between us was strong and vibrant. By total surprise, I got my bookkeeping job back at Escuela Hispana Montessori, and Sheila got deeply involved in education—in fact studying the Montessori method and interning at Escuela.

We no longer were part of the meat co-op. Sheila became a quasi-vegetarian and no longer ate meat. Allowing herself poultry and seafood, she focused primarily on whole grains and vegetables. While I still ate meat occasionally, I resurrected my love for basketball, and began to play pickup games at various playgrounds. My huffing and puffing on the playground dictated to me that I needed to reduce or eliminate my smoking, which I accomplished with surprising ease.

While in the process of trying to stop smoking, I was saddled with vivid and painful dreams. In one, I was drinking in solitude on one side of the bar, while my friends were whooping it up, smoking and drinking on the other side. In another, I saw them driving and smoking in a convertible car, the wind ruffling their hair, while I was standing alone on the sidewalk. The dreams lasted for about a year, but the increased stamina I felt while shooting hoops more than offset these disturbing scenarios.

By the beginning of 1974, Sheila had completed her Montessori certification program and took her first teaching job at West Side Montessori, a progressive pre-school that was founded by a half a dozen families in the 1960s. She came home every afternoon gushing with energy and excitement about her three-year-olds and their antics.

Strong friendships blossomed from working with colleagues who, in true character of the 1960s, were multi-dimensional. Their backgrounds were diverse. One had a psychology background, another was a caterer, but they were all drawn to early childhood education, feeling a need to make a difference. Many received advanced degrees in education, as Sheila did.

25

I was determined to maintain my current lifestyle, but wasn't going anywhere. With my long thinning hair, and wild mustache intact, I continued to work part time, smoke weed, play basketball and wanted to believe that I was still "on top of the moment". The sunshine was gone; I began to feel more and more isolated and disconnected from myself, so much so, that it affected my sleep.

The walls seemed to shake at night, not just metaphorically, but literally because the bar below us had new ownership and shifted from great jazz to Latin disco.

At about three AM every morning, a booming microphone announced, "last dance", and suddenly the music amped up and the walls vibrated. There was an uncontrollable vibration running inside of me as well, as wave after wave of anxiety washed through my chest and stomach, making it difficult to breathe. This happened primarily at night, when I was trying to drift into sleep.

At times, it would also come on without warning during the day. I could not eat for fear that I would suffocate and at night when I finally fell asleep, I feared that I would not wake up. This fear, which I was always able to tuck away and hide neatly inside fissures of my soul, now reigned unchecked, like a punishing wind across a barren landscape.

I began to feel increasingly vulnerable. I felt porous and defenseless, as if air could pass through me and I feared I would be overcome. I felt as though I had no body, that I was ethereal, losing substance, and susceptible to anything and everything. I read an article about rape in a men's prison and had a visceral reaction to it, visualizing that it could happen to me.

The winter of 1974, we visited Amsterdam—as we did every year until 1980. While crossing a heavily trafficked street, I asked my mother to take my arm so I could guide her. She said, with an annoyed tone, "I don't need you; I can cross the street by myself." She may very well have said the exact same words before, or maybe I heard them for the first time.

In any case, I felt like my head was ripped open and my brain was oozing out onto the cobblestoned street. My childhood had prepared me to function well on a landscape filled with moving objects; like the dancing bear, I was trained to dodge the bullets. But, I was not ready for this. I felt profoundly rejected, disoriented, and angry. Didn't she realize that I was her prince, her advocate and her protector? Now I felt gutted, diminished and demoralized.

A couple of months went by and I remained in the same dark place. If it wasn't for Sheila, who knows where this would have gone. I asked her to stay awake every night until I fell asleep. Somehow, Sheila's love and patience gave me a sliver of serenity, so that I could sleep for a little while. Wine, which I had always loved, now served another purpose. It became a form of daily self-medication, dulling my senses, while continuing to be a celebration for my tongue and mouth. I realized that these actions were simply band aids and that I needed help.

I had never been in therapy. Whether it was out of fear of what might be found out or the macho myth that real men didn't need outside help, I loathed and despised the idea of therapy. I believed it was self-indulgent, that you solved your own problems, with the support of your partner or, at worst, your family.

I was dubious about the whole therapy process and this prolonged my agony until I saw no other way. Fortunately, both Marja and Sheila, separately, had been in therapy with the same therapist, Millie. The fact that the two people dearest to me knew a therapist first hand, was all important and made my decision easier.

A short, plump woman with intelligent eyes, inviting smile and sharp sense of wit greeted me at her front door. Millie's apartment had many small rooms with high ceilings, lots of books and fresh-cut flowers. Her work space looked more like a living room than an office, with a loveseat sofa, two comfortable chairs, a coffee table, a standing lamp, and several ash trays. Millie's simpatico and *élan* made the setting even more comfortable, as if I were visiting an old friend.

After my initial visit during which I described my background, my recent experience with my mother, my confusion and vulnerability, I met with her again. Therapy felt more like a game of cards where one observed the other player for clues about their state of being, before revealing something about one's self.

The process did not feel real to me and at some point, maybe in our fifth session, I felt as though we were dueling mentally. I believed that I was more intelligent and my sense of superiority or intellect served as a wall, rather than a gateway, into the realm of the subconscious. I was defensive and did not trust anyone else to guide me, yet I did understand that I needed to continue therapy.

It was clear to me that as much as I wanted to heal myself, that I could not do it alone. During one session I asked about group therapy as an alternative to our individual sessions. The dynamic of a group, though emotionally risky, appealed to me because I trusted groups more readily than individuals.

I recalled my kibbutz experiences and how my friendships within a communal environment replaced the family nucleus and turned out to be supportive and nurturing. My first group session was more like a parody of the Bob Newhart show, which revolved around his therapy practice and the neurotic patients he listened to.

I felt as though I was hovering above the room, peering at these people relating their trivial problems, and questioned why I was there. As I did under most circumstances, I observed the room, watched the clock, and studied the faces of each person (including Millie's) and how they interacted within the group.

Then suddenly, I was asked, by one of the group, "So Joe, tell us about yourself?" The sudden question, without any warning, made me scramble for words, as I tried to collect myself. I joked, "I am here to gather information for the Bob Newhart Show." Silence followed, and Millie tried to shift the attention to another participant, but the person who had asked the question angrily retorted, "That's not funny, and don't waste our time."

Beet red, cornered with no place to hide, I apologized, just as Millie announced the end of the session. I left her apartment and scurried down the stairs to avoid the awkwardness of small talk on the elevator and my embarrassment for acting inappropriately.

I forced myself to go back the following week. Each week, at least for the first few months, was a revelation. I was astounded to find myself at times crying, venting in anger or profoundly touched by what someone else said. It seemed like an archeological dig where each week I discovered a new layer, revealing a mosaic of my feelings. I began to experience emotions, other than anger. At first, these feelings felt unreal, but eventually I owned them and gained confidence that they were real and part of me.

26

Six months had passed since anxiety had taken control of my life. I weighed less than I did in high school and veins were nearly visible in my biceps, yet I was making progress. My nightly anxiety waves were shorter, I felt that I could breathe without gagging, and I continued to participate in the group therapy sessions. No longer was I the outsider. I knew as much about each person as he or she was willing to share, and I appreciated the dynamic of the group and its commitment to honesty, without ceremony.

In that setting, I was able to expose my feelings. I talked about my sense of loss, of abandonment and my lost innocence. I revealed my inability to differentiate between pity and love, between anger and depression.

Until I entered group therapy, I could not focus on the anger I felt towards my parents, most notably my mother. I was terrified to face my anger towards them. How could I be angry at them, after all they had gone through?! They had to send me away, for my safety as well as theirs, I rationalized. But, they had done more, they took me away from Moeder and Vader, and without malice, robbed me of my childhood.

It was not until I dealt with the anger I felt towards my mother that I made progress. At first, the anger towards her felt forced, but with time, effort, and support from the group, it began to feel real. The anger was washed with tears of joy, anguish, and self-pity.

It also opened me to the feelings of love. No longer a frozen slab of marble, I was thawing out, able to distinguish my feelings and bursting with new vitality and hope. Not too surprisingly, our annual trips to Holland became more difficult. My anger towards my mom made these brief gatherings awkward and bitter.

Concurrently, though my parents had moved to Amsterdam to be nearer to our extended family, they felt more and more lonely. Like many other WWII survivors they were damaged, lived solely through their children and were psychologically unable to develop their own paths, interests or friendships. This created a dilemma for both myself and Marja. Although we wished them well, we, surprisingly, found the separation to be therapeutic. It lifted a burden we had carried since childhood.

We weren't ready for them to come back to New York, even though the Dutch government had changed its guidelines for WWII reparation eligibility. Now, recipients no longer needed to live in the country of their birth, but could return to the countries they had adopted. When our parents approached us about returning to the US, with trepidation and awkwardness, I told them that we needed more time apart from them. The fragile child in me wasn't ready to forgive and forget. To our surprise, they did not go against our wishes and dutifully remained in Holland for another five years.

Anger and pity were no longer the only feelings I experienced. Love and empathy created a new balance for me. Skyscrapers cannot be built on quicksand, nor could my personal development be achieved without reducing my combustible anger. Through trial and error and even mechanically counting to ten before responding, my subterranean anger slowly subsided. Although mistakes were landmines that needed to be avoided at all cost, I became less rigid and tried to tolerate my mistakes, and those of others.

With anger becoming more sporadic and less explosive, I experienced the vicissitudes of depression. For the first time, I no longer viewed myself as the last of the buccaneers, but instead as someone who was only good enough to wash toilets, a perspective which disturbed me deeply. Of course, neither of these self-images truly represented me, since they were extreme opposites. I resisted change.

I cherished my wild mustache and long hair and treasured being hidden in our tenement home. When an opportunity arose that would allow us to move two blocks north to an apartment building with an elevator, I envisioned that it was a move "uptown". The idea of recognizing and greeting people in the hallway and elevator, holding doors open and helping people carry their shopping bags, all the hallmarks of good neighborliness and citizenship, were an anathema to me.

I believed that these conventions would weigh me down and enslave me once more, diminishing my spirit as it did when I was forced to work after school each day at age fifteen. Sheila, on the other hand, was ready to move into an "adult" apartment, especially since it was affordable, rent stabilized and most importantly, had rooms with doors.

The transition from the tenement to the apartment building was less traumatic than I thought it would be. Our sixth-floor two-bedroom apartment was sunny, had oak parquet floors, an eat-in kitchen plus an actual bathroom. The furniture and carpeting we brought over was scattered as deftly as we could, but you could still hear an echo whenever we spoke or moved about. Two elderly spinster sisters lived below us and, bothered by our movements in the apartment, banged on their ceiling to let us know their displeasure.

Outside of our cantankerous neighbors below, I quickly learned to tolerate the elevator greetings and small talk. In fact, we became part of a group of neighborhood people who formed the Good Food Co-op, a food co-op that is still functioning today. Moreover, I helped Saylor, our neighbor and the quintessential good citizen, to mulch the trees on our block. Living in our new home brought about some obvious and subtle changes in my life.

My mustache and long hair, which until then were my façade, my symbol of rebellion, counter-culture, and independence, now felt like a glued-on mask. I felt inhibited by it. Symbolically, no fresh air could enter and I felt imprisoned by it. One night I could bare it no longer and unbeknownst to Sheila, I slowly, painstakingly, removed the mustache. At first the thick mustache resisted the razor, but eventually succumbed. It was astonishing how this small alteration changed my appearance. I looked like a different person.

The following morning Sheila shrieked with anger to find a different person in her bed. Her anger stemmed as much from not being told what I was planning, as from the radical difference it made in my appearance. Soon thereafter my long locks were sheared as well, but this time I gave Sheila plenty of notice. The mask ripped off, exposed me to new ideas, risk taking and heightened my sense of self awareness. A new face, no longer hidden.

Whether it was the move to the apartment building, the results of therapy, or simply waking out of a slumber, I no longer wanted to live on the edges of everyday life, hiding within my own shadow and state of victimhood. Instead, I wanted to complete myself, regardless of the risks involved.

As my confidence grew and I understood myself more fully, I wanted to grow in other ways, to gain new skills, find meaningful work and start a family. But, what kind of work did I want to do?! I enjoyed management, bookkeeping and accounting, but hated the idea of "business".

My work experience was tainted by feelings of servitude and enslavement to my parents, by the boredom felt while doing mundane tasks, the narrowmindedness of fellow workers, and the general concept of making a profit. Flustered, I found it difficult to visualize what direction was best for me.

During one of my therapy sessions, I shared this dilemma with my group. Someone who worked as an executive "head hunter", said, "You mentioned that you were good in business matters and enjoyed working in day care centers and Head Start. Why not find a full-time job in a school, possibly as a business manager?" The title, Business Manager, Finance Director or Chief Financial Officer, was a revelation. I mulled it over.

The image of an accountant felt too straight and narrow, being a bookkeeper felt demeaning, but business manager sounded just right. I had always enjoyed a nurturing school environment with people who had dreams and interests that I could identify with and whose collective purpose was to guide and support the development of children.

PART 5

AMERICA 1977 - PRESENT

27

"Welcome to Westside Montessori", the director, Penny, stated with a shy, crooked smile. It was 1977, and I was hired as the business manager of the private pre-school on the upper west side where Sheila worked. The school was considered a "limited purchase of service" school because in addition to parents who paid full tuition, it enrolled families who paid lower fees, scaled to their family income.

The school was reimbursed monthly by New York State Child Development Agency for the disparity between the parental fees and the tuition rate for a full-paying child.

As a result, the school's revenue was stable, while the whole school community was enriched by the diversity of its student body. As part of the interview process, I met with the director, a group of administrators and the Chair of the Finance Committee.

The interview experience enlightened me to the practices of the private (independent) school world. Unlike most other school roles, I understood that I was not only hired by and accountable to the director, but also needed to be responsible to the Board of Trustees.

As a result, I held allegiance to not just one person or entity, but to the entire school. I not only carried a reverence for the children, teachers, staff, parents, and philosophy, but for the whole gestalt. This community became my extended family and, like the kibbutz, I felt respected and recognized. I loved it.

The fact that Sheila worked there, was a mixed blessing, especially for her. There was some tension between the administration and teachers over salary and work conditions, and my administrative presence made matters awkward for her.

No doubt that was the primary reason she left a year later and began work as a director of a day care facility in a mid-town settlement house. But, while she was at Westside, I often stopped into her class and made-up stories, spontaneously for the children, who sat in rapt attention.

A favorite was a story about a cyclops who lived in a cave. I asked my audience, "Who stayed outside and who went in?" The children, based on their curiosity or fear chose one or the other, with a few changing their minds midway and entered my narration with their own ideas.

In my new career, story-telling became part of my experience, along with the more mundane, sobering responsibilities of finance, resource and facilities management. I envisioned being in the center of the school, not high on a perch like an unapproachable financial eagle, but one who impacted all constituencies, as they impacted me.

Not every school has an organizational style that supports multi-faceted roles or allows administrative staff to participate in the educational stream of the school. There is little understanding that each person, whether a custodian, teacher or administrator, is a role model whose actions are noticed by children. Each person working around children has a responsibility that goes well beyond his or her narrow job descriptions, and each should ask, "How will my statements or actions impact the watchful child."

I took my responsibilities seriously, as I had done throughout my life, and although I felt accomplished, it came with a price. In my efforts to competently complete every task and responsibility, came also the concern that I would make mistakes.

In my psyche mistakes were still *"verboden"*, and potentially fatal. The angst I felt when I made a mistake, especially at work, were akin to being "found out", possibly being ostracized by the community and excommunicated.

Sadly, whenever Sheila would remind me that everyone makes mistakes and that it's part of the learning process, she inadvertently threw gas on the smoldering fire inside of me. To mitigate this angst, I would bring home my briefcase filled with current work.

For the first two years, I dutifully accomplished as much work at home as was necessary to ensure that I felt satisfied and worthy, and that I would be able to sleep that night. Curiously, the more I was deemed competent and well-prepared by my colleagues and those I was accountable to, the less extra work I would do at home.

The placement of my briefcase in the apartment designated how much I actually accomplished at home. At first, it was planted next to my desk in the bedroom, a year later it was in the living room and finally it was left unopened in the vestibule, near the front door. It served as an organizational life lesson for me, because I learned to work in a binary way, where one pile needed completion within a specific time frame, while the other pile was more open ended and could be worked on, or not, at my leisure.

As with most small entities, especially of the not-for-profit variety, the organizational roles are driven more by charisma than through the traditional corporate model. When Penny left Westside Montessori, it created a vacuum that was difficult to fill. The new director brought different strengths, weaknesses and vision, and the school tried to embrace those differences. I realized early on that the new director's skill base overlapped with mine, and that she had a clear interest in administrative management.

Westside was a small school, and I understood that inadvertently my role was being diminished as the director took more and more interest in the various business aspects that I would normally tackle. To me, timing is everything. Waiting too long to act could—at minimum—spell boredom, anger, professional emasculation or in my maternal grandmother's case, death. Reluctantly, the following year I decided to look for another job.

El Barrio is considered the far east, as compared to the Upper Westside where Westside Montessori was located, and in many ways the economic and cultural gap was even wider. The neighborhood surrounding Westside consisted of co-op apartment buildings, town houses, Riverside Park and a few SRO hotels, mostly representing Manhattan affluence. El Barrio is made up of concrete and brick housing projects, tenements, bodegas, and no parks of consequence.

On this day, I found myself on 104th Street and Third Avenue looking for the offices of the Union Settlement Association, where I had an interview. Union Settlement was founded in 1895, by members of Union Theological Seminary, to serve the needs of immigrants and the poor.

I was interviewed by the Executive Director, and the Board of Trustees which included such luminaries as Cyrus Vance, who had just finished a term as Secretary of State under President Carter, and Frederick Schwarz Jr., Corporation Counsel to Mayor Koch and great grandson of the founder of the toy company, F.A.O Schwarz.

I felt totally intimidated by the illustrious trustees, and because I knew little about multi-program record keeping and its administrative management, felt inadequate. It was an in-depth interview and included questions concerning Sheila and our relationship.

The interview process lasted for several weeks, and though friendly in tone, it felt more like an interrogation. Ultimately my lack of multi-program experience proved to be the sticking point, and I was not offered the job. I felt enormous relief and, although the interview process made me extremely tense, I was proud that I was one of two final candidates for the position.

A few months thereafter, in early July 1980, I met Joyce McCray. It was a smoldering, hot day and I was interviewing for the Business Manager position at Friends Seminary. Here was the Head of School, arms folded across her chest, talking to me from behind a curtain of cigarette smoke. She seemed to tower over me and pummeled me with insightful questions. I was then interviewed by various administrators and met with Joyce a second time that afternoon. As she stood up I could see, to my surprise, that she was a rather small woman.

Months later, I realized that these initial impressions were the very essence of Joyce: her towering intelligence, sharp wit, intuitive timing, and boundless energy fused into a tiny frame. She was a global thinker who took the time to focus on the smallest of details. During administrative retreats, she would play tennis in the morning, have a productive meeting in the afternoon, outdrink everyone that evening and somewhere in between bake three different pies for brunch the following day. Fiercely loyal to family and friends, she could be equally critical and dismissive of people she didn't care for. Her friends and colleagues became her extended family and she easily interwove her private life with that of the school.

I was in awe of her. To me she seemed like an Olympian goddess, who easily flowed from her Corinthian temple to the town and its people below. I had never met anyone like her before, and through her, peeked into another world, a Protestant upper middle-class world that I was not privy to. I was like a little boy, nose pressed to the window glass looking into the candy store with all its treats, conscious of my separateness.

28

Friends Seminary, a Quaker co-educational school, had already been in existence for over one hundred and ninety years by the time I arrived. Even in its earliest days on Elizabeth Street, the founding elders understood that for the school to survive and grow, they would have to open enrollment to non-Quakers. In fact, it wasn't long before Quaker students were a minority, if not a fraction of the total enrollment. This meant that the Quaker Board had to be more vigilant in demonstrating Quaker practices than other Friends' schools, where the Quaker enrollment was dominant or much more substantial than in NYC. As a result, instead of being focused on fundraising like most other Boards, Friends Seminary focused on policy making.

When I arrived at the school, there was no traditional endowment fund. Instead they had a very tiny "Board Designated Endowment" of less than $220,000. Despite that, under Joyce's leadership, the school quickly became successful. On the other hand, the quest for financial stability, though much better, has remained an ongoing goal.

1980 was a watershed year, not only because my job at Friends had crystalized what my career path would be, but it was also the year my parents returned from Holland. My healing process was in full swing and I no longer needed a distance from them.

The anger towards my mother, which had consumed me throughout my life, had subsided. I was finally able to forgive and let go of that emotionally stained blanket that had covered my heart for so long. I wanted to share my life with them in a way I never could before. I had made important strides in therapy, Sheila was pregnant, and we looked forward to sharing our excitement with my parents. They were also more determined than ever to return to the States, as were uncle Jules and aunt Emmy. I had matured, was about to become a father, was proud of my job, and now could welcome mommy and poppy with open arms.

My parents moved to Starrett City, a Brooklyn housing complex in East New York that seemed to attract young families and families who had recently arrived in the US. In that way, it replicated their experience at Bijlmermeer in Amsterdam. Like Bijlmermeer, Starrett City was a vibrant community for a limited time. It lost its luster as soon as the immigrants created stable lives and the young families, planning to have children, moved to more attractive neighborhoods or the suburbs.

The housing fell into decline, and became less attractive. For my parents, their apartment served as a comfortable "holding bin" that allowed them to see their children and grandchildren. They had no interest or involvement in the community, other than the supermarket where they shopped and the pharmacy where they filled their prescriptions, and where my father bought cigarillos. It was as though they helicoptered from the roof of Starrett City to other parts of Brooklyn or Manhattan to see Marja or me—oblivious of everything in between.

Concurrently, Sheila and I were renting a summer bungalow in

Dutchess County near Beacon, NY, that we traveled to each weekend. It was a simple, comfortable, two-bedroom cottage, modestly furbished, on a grassy knoll, surrounded by other bungalows. It typified a bungalow colony in that it had a recreation hall, and pool.

At one time, it was considered a socialist leaning summer bungalow colony, but by the time Sheila and I learned about it through Marja, it no longer held that cache and was simply a nice, reasonably priced respite, ninety minutes from the city, offering a taste of country living. The closeness of the bungalows to one another, gave the colony an intimacy and sense of community that was truly unique. Marja had a bungalow, and a year or two later our parents rented one as well, creating a "kibbutz" like environment that was pleasing to all of us. Marja's sons, Steven and Brian, were thirteen and seven respectively, and could move about the property unsupervised, visiting us or Oma and Opa whenever they wished.

The sweet summer contrasted sharply with the previous summer, which was filled with depression, detachment and numbness. After six weeks of quiet excitement about her pregnancy, shared only with Marja, Sheila miscarried. She mourned her loss and in anger, metaphorically lashed out at her own body for failing her.

To me, the pregnancy and miscarriage weren't real. I had no emotional connection to the fetus, its early growth, or sudden demise. It had been a dream, a wish, and then it was gone. I tried to support Sheila as best as I could, but felt guilty that I did not feel any loss myself. After visiting her obstetrician, we both gained greater insight as to why miscarriages occur and when it was appropriate to begin anew.

A few months after that sad event, while watching a film about World War II, where a bewildered young boy stood next to his suitcase while people were being packed onto the trains, I suddenly burst into tears and quietly wailed uncontrollably. Clearly, my grief was for the little boy inside of me, but also for the loss of a child unformed.

As the obstetrician had foreseen, Sheila became pregnant very quickly, and although we both worried throughout the pregnancy, everything developed normally with no signs of miscarriage. By the end of the first trimester, our obstetrician told us that she wasn't happy with the color of the amniotic fluid removed during the amniocentesis test, although it would take weeks before we received the definitive results.

Alarmed and slightly hysterical, we immediately searched for a second opinion. We found a high-risk obstetrician who came with sterling references. He solved the mystery of the dark amniotic fluid within minutes. He correctly surmised that it had to do with blood in the amniotic fluid, which was a common occurrence. The test results a few weeks later confirmed his diagnosis and the pregnancy proceeded normally. With the shift in doctors, also came a change of hospitals. We were now affiliated with Mount Sinai, and were much happier with their facilities and services.

After eight months of pregnancy, we decided to get married, a decision that occurred after weeks of arguing. I feared that if for any reason Sheila and I were to separate, I would not have equal access to our child. In this male-dominated culture, it is ironic that custody issues lean heavily in favor of the mother.

Sheila, who had been married before, was against marrying again. In deference to my concerns and the recognition that insurance coverage for a family was cheaper than having two individual plans, she acquiesced. The day we married, Sheila met me at Friends Seminary, Joyce and the administrative team ceremoniously threw rice at us and cheered. There was a visible quality of comic desperation to this scene, since I was on crutches and Sheila was eight months pregnant.

I had recently broken my ankle playing basketball, and this

comedic scene was dramatically displayed while we waited in a long line at City Hall. After the civil ceremony we proceeded to Sheila's therapist's office, where her therapist, who was also a minister, officiated. Marja was there, as well as several friends. Sheila and I said some very nice things to one another. The short, intimate ceremony was followed by a lovely lunch with our friends, who wished us well.

For a couple who already had lived together for eleven years, this day was pleasant, but not a profound experience. The truly profound moment was eleven years earlier, when we first met, began to live together, formed our relationship and built our nest. When people ask us how long we have we been married, we answer that we have been together since September 1970. That is the anniversary we recognize.

About the same time, after twenty years of eligibility, I decided to become a naturalized citizen. As a green card holder (alien resident), I never felt confident about the permanency of my residence in the US. I always believed that under certain circumstances, I might be deported. Citizenship allowed me to believe that our young family would not be undermined by forced deportation. But, the primary impetus for naturalization was my maturation. I wanted to stop running and hiding and no longer felt comfortable sitting on the fence, like a Greek, sullenly watching the Romans at work and play. Instead, I wanted to participate on an equal footing.

My world vision had expanded and I now participated in life. I was willing to compromise, to adapt and to grow. If I had not come to that consciousness, I would have petrified and my life cycle would have frozen in state.

My political perspectives also changed. I was no longer rigid in my views and I no longer saw issues as black or white. Instead, though I continued to identify with left wing causes, there were times when my response was more like a conservative's. The freedom to think and act on what I believed in, while always being aware of my impact on others, became an important aspect of how I conducted myself in daily life.

The taxi ride to Mount Sinai seemed extremely slow, and Sheila was in agony. Her contractions suggested that the baby no longer wanted to float in amniotic fluid, but to inhale fresh air. At the hospital, we were told that she wasn't sufficiently dilated, but they suggested that she should stay because the baby was already two weeks late. Ultimately, Sheila received an epidural to relieve the pain, and after 14 hours, she was dilated sufficiently and I saw the crown of the baby's head.

Jacob was born on May 30th, 1981, a quiet, lazy Saturday morning. He was beautiful, except that the umbilical cord was wrapped around his neck like a baby boa. Within a matter of seconds, the doctor introduced clips, cut the cord, and the reassuring sound of Jacob's crying was heard.

Sheila and I were ever thankful that we chose a high-risk doctor, who knew exactly what to do. Later, out of exhaustion and restlessness, I stared through the window of the nursery and saw all the babies born that day. I guessed that most of them were born early or prematurely, because their heads seemed dented in a little, or something seemed awry in their faces, or they seemed small. It could also be that I thought my own son was perfect, and every other baby was wrinkled.

I was utterly amazed by the ocean of feelings I felt towards this tiny being. Until the birth, I wasn't sure how I would feel towards my child. Until then, my only experience was my love for Sheila, which certainly was not instantaneous. I left the hospital a few hours later, Sheila was asleep, my son was swaddled tightly in the nursery, and I breathed in the city air deeply. To me it smelled like perfume.

As I went home, I reflected on the blissful event and what it meant to me. Eleven years before, when Sheila and I talked about anything and everything, I mentioned that I envisioned a Sicilian-sized family. I hoped that we would have many children, possibly five or six. I could see them sitting around a dining room table with me at one end and Sheila at the other. Whether I envisioned that out of seeing old films or felt compelled to accomplish this as a punch to Hitler's face, I didn't know.

But as with all grand schemes, I started large and then modified my goals to what was more realistic. Besides, Sheila, did not want more than three children, and by the late 1980s I realized that it would be quite an economic struggle to support even Sheila's vision.

The fact that our child was a boy filled me with paternal pride. The knowledge and security that the Gosler name would live on in this universe was extremely important to me. Even though Jake's surname is officially Wolper-Gosler, as opposed to just Gosler, I felt I was honoring both my parents and the numerous cousins, aunts, uncles and grandparents that had been murdered during WWII.

I was also intent on being an everyday dad, not just a weekend dad. As much as I loved my own father with his few words and big heart, I never saw him as a true dad. My father was never involved in the day-to-day events of my life. He was not a strong male role model. I yearned for a father who would have my back, someone to share my experiences with, someone who would guide me.

I was determined to be directly involved with my son, to schedule doctor appointments, make his meals, worry about him, play with him, guide him and love him. I understood that I would be an "in-your-face" kind of dad, and that the excesses of my shadow might ruffle his wings.

My own childhood experiences and relationship with my father did not allow me to create an ideal balance between being absent or ever-present. I had to be the complete, opposite of my father. I hoped that this dialectic would someday allow my son, as a father, to choose a role in between these two extremes.

I returned to work a week after Jake's birth, and was greeted with a phone call, "Hello Mr. Gosler, this is Union Settlement. Are you still interested in the job we listed...?" I was flabbergasted, and responded, "Let me get back to you tomorrow". The more I thought about the offer, the tenser I became. This was an important crossroad for me.

The path I had chosen meant that I would be serving upper middle income and affluent families, while the path initially not offered was one serving poor and lower income families. My mind leaned towards serving the poor, but whether due to my growing family, quality of the workplace or the comfort of being close to home, I chose to stay at Friends. The choice paid dividends not only because the school and community and most notably its Quaker beliefs would enrich me deeply and guide me throughout my life, but also because it allowed for an entrepreneurial plunge that would not have happened if I had accepted the "offer".

Not only had I chosen my career path on that yellow brick road, but something else had become clear and changed as well. The many lashes from Nazi Germany that had broken my parents' spirit, and almost an entire people's, left their sting on me as well.

Since childhood, the dual feelings of loss and suffering that molded me into a victim and had been part of my self-image, had shifted. The more I acted in the arena of everyday life, collaborated, competed and made friends, the more fulfilled and less isolated I became. And the less I sulked. In fact, I found it difficult to tolerate people who felt sorry for themselves. I saw the vapors of victimhood as corrosive to the human spirit and believed that one should try to get free of that quagmire as soon as he could, or avoid it completely, if possible.

Sadly, there are many people who prefer to live in that state, because like an old raggedy blanket, it is familiar and warm. I found that such people often use their energy and skills to remain victimized, rather than attempting to change their lives. Thus, they have no moral compass, have difficulty developing or maintaining anything positive in their lives, and by circumstance are not trustworthy. I was glad to leave such a community behind, and rarely trespassed through it again. This is not to say that I don't have empathy for victims, I just believe that victimhood shouldn't define who you are.

My decision to remain at Friends Seminary, also meant that I became more involved in other aspects of school life. Whether it was related to self-healing or my nurturing instincts, I chaperoned the eight and nine-year-olds on their annual trip to the Poconos. I coached middle-school baseball, participated in school plays and joined the faculty-student basketball tournaments. In the late 1990s, I was co-Principal pro-temp for a month. The school was the missing community I had always longed for.

Most importantly I spoke to students and faculty at assemblies about my experiences as a hidden child. In preparation for these assemblies, I wrote a synopsis of my experience during WWII. Sharing my story was liberating. My goal was to convey that each person has a story to tell and that we must all struggle to overcome that which holds us down. The responses from faculty and students, through their questions, tears and empathy, were an affirmation that my "voice" mattered.

No matter how often I read my story, there is always some word or sentence that triggers a tremor in my voice. I slow down until the emotion passes. Just a reminder that old wounds never fully heal.

Many of the faculty were drawn to Friends because of the Quaker practices and beliefs. The belief in the importance of the individual within a community, the inner light within each person, worshipping in silence, pacifism, conflict resolution and simplicity, felt right to me as well.

The Quaker ethic peeled away the politics of everyday life and replaced it with an empathy and clear sightedness that was unique and impactful. It resonated with me that much more, because my own form of communication and business practices paralleled many Quaker practices. I was drawn to the culture of the school and thrived within its community. As my career blossomed, I decided to go back to school and get an MBA.

The MBA degree proved to be of no consequence in the pursuit of career advancement. Although I was wooed by two different schools, I never had any interest in pursuing another job, whether in a for profit or not-for-profit setting. The MBA program did, however, offer new insights into creative business practices that enriched my management skills at Friends. Most importantly, it prepared me for the joint venture which Sheila and I soon developed.

29

Even prior to Jacob's birth, Sheila and I had fantasized about starting a pre-school on the Lower East Side. When we walked in the neighborhood, we noticed that there weren't any quality nursery schools in evidence. There were a few day care centers, where a family could drop off their young ones and pick them up later in the day when they returned from work or school, but these were focused on parental support more than on what the children needed. We wanted to focus totally on children's needs. "Beginnings a Toddler Program" began with 5 toddlers in our apartment.

With five or fewer toddlers there were no licensing requirements, but for our own protection, we childproofed our apartment, purchased a high level of liability insurance and hired an assistant to work with Sheila.

We planned to do this for two years in our apartment, limit our costs, save some money, and gain the experience necessary to find an appropriate location to start a nursery school. An irate neighbor who lived below us accelerated the process, and six months after we began, we were forced to look for a rental space.

Through pure luck, I found a place that was equidistant between Grace Church School and Friends Seminary, the two schools we hoped our young graduates would attend. Located on East 16th Street and Irving Place, it was the edge of Gramercy Park and fortuitously had previously housed a pre-school.

We opened in September 1984 with 15 half-day children. Sheila was the director, teacher and troubleshooter. I negotiated contracts, developed budgets, did the record keeping, and cleaned the two classrooms between the morning and afternoon programs during my lunch break at Friends.

The loft-size space, divided into three separate rooms, was licensed for 35 full-time children, at any given time. Each year, Beginnings grew. In 1989, we rented a second floor, and the total number of children throughout the day, with morning and afternoon programs grew to 140.

After graduating from Beginnings many children attended independent schools in Manhattan and Brooklyn or specialized TAG (talented & gifted) public schools. The division of labor had changed as dramatically with the growth in enrollment. There were more teachers, assistants, several administrators, a receptionist and a custodian. It was no longer the sweet fantasy of "our little school", but a thriving business supporting a community. The larger it became, the larger the responsibilities were, and the more nervous I became.

Managing cash-flow is the hallmark of small businesses. Will we have enough cash to make payroll, pay off the renovation bills, meet next month's rent, or will I need to borrow funds from my TIAA retirement plan?

These were ongoing and agonizing worries that plagued me

throughout. The fear and terror of not meeting my responsibilities to others at times consumed me, in a way all too familiar. I am sure I was not the only small businessman to feel this way, but few would have taken it to the extremes that I did. It was not until fifteen years later that I became less anxious about the school, when I realized that Beginnings' had a life of its own and could take care of itself.

30

Although Jake, our son, could have attended Beginnings, we believed that it would be confusing for him. How could his mommy also be his teacher? That would be too difficult for a two-year-old to handle emotionally. As a result, he went to a nursery school in SOHO, called the Children's Energy Center. Each day I put Jake in the stroller and we made our way to the Center on Thompson Street, and Sheila picked him up after teaching.

As with many new parents, this was a time when Sheila and I insulated ourselves from the rest of the world and focused our attention on Jake. The word "rendezvous", that romantic notion of meeting somewhere by ourselves left our vocabulary.

It was a time when I drank wine more regularly, sang opera, gained weight, and had chronic backaches. In fact, I joked that the backaches occurred because of giving birth to Jake. I was so connected to Jake. My son was my pride, and he represented victory over death and my dark beginnings. Sometimes, we would have group hugs, when either Sheila or I carried Jake. We would embrace and chant, "Hug, Hug, Hug", as Jake was gently smothered with love. At other times, in a similar embrace, we would slow dance to a Frank Sinatra song. These were innocent, magical times!

About a year later, on a routine stroller trip to his nursery school, Jake mentioned that his friend Jack lived in a building near his school. He described him as a tall man, that he saw a lot, and even pointed to the building where Jack lived. SOHO and all of NYC, if not beyond, was still reeling from the disappearance five years earlier of a boy, named Etan Patz. I swallowed deeply, and in my paranoia and concern, I lingered outside the School, after I dropped Jake at the Center.

My vigilance subsided once I learned that it was quite common for children of three to invent an imaginary friend and a separate universe, that they alone could enter and exit, much like my treehouse in Israel. I was much more protective as a parent than Sheila, not just in terms of protecting Jake from potential harm, but even when it came to dressing him appropriately for inclement weather. I worried about many things, but I was even more obsessive when it related to my son.

On the other hand, when it came to sports I was much more of a risk-taker. After all, sports are games with parameters and appropriate gear. I didn't think twice about rolling a hard baseball to Jake when he was not yet three. It rolled under his glove, up his leg and stomach and hit his chin. The surprise and sudden pain, made him cry a little, but he soon became familiar and comfortable throwing and catching the baseball.

A few years later, when Jake played in Little League, he was already a "consummate" player, and although he became a three-season athlete at Friends, baseball remained his passion. It was an activity that Jake and I enjoyed together, and the discussion of baseball history, teams, players, and stats developed a dialect and intimacy that we both truly loved.

To me, Manhattan was like a village. Not only did I live twelve blocks from my work place, but Jake began attending Friends Seminary at age four, and Sheila worked a block further west. My whole world, my family, was within the radius of a single block. I could peer in through the small window in the classroom's wooden door and see my son working on a project with a few other children, or from a distance, watch him in the gym. Naturally, this level of intimacy became awkward for Jake when he started 7th grade, when, more often than not, he would avoid me as he saw me coming down the corridor. But for the most part, it worked out to his advantage, especially when he could shake down his pop after school for some money.

On alternate Fridays, I opened the school. I unlocked the metal gates that led to the school entrance, and with Jake at my side, turn off the alarms, while Jake, stretching up on his toes, turned on the Meeting House lights. When administrators and receptionists arrived, we would go to Joe Juniors, the corner coffee shop, sit at the counter and have breakfast together. The painful memories of my family's diaspora, the murder of my relatives, the scattering of those who remained, were all nullified by these delicious experiences, and I was ever thankful that I had chosen to remain at Friends rather than taken the "offer".

Life pulsated forward and my career was taking off. I had a fresh minted MBA that gave me the legitimacy I felt I had lacked. Beginnings was thriving, Marja was doing well, and my parents were enjoying Jake. But, even paradise is never perfect. My father had malignant tumors on his lungs. He didn't believe in preventive medicine. His generation avoided medical care, until there was no recourse but to see a doctor. He had lost a definite amount of weight, felt weak, and only through my mother's lobbying finally saw a doctor. After a battery of tests, he was diagnosed with stage-three lung cancer and diabetes. The latter was most surprising because he was never aware of any symptoms. But the cancer diagnosis was even more shocking. Although he smoked cigarettes, he had never inhaled.

I thought that the many evenings he spent asleep in his easy chair, inhaling the smoke from the Cigarello that dangled from his mouth precariously, was the cause of the cancer. But, it could easily have been the asbestos that insulated the water pipes in the chicken coops, or the plastic fiber he may have inhaled while working in the garment industry, or maybe something totally unrelated.

The three of us often visited my parents in Starrett City to spend time with my ailing father. He would chat with Jake about school and the NY Mets. "And how is Strawberry, or Doc doing", he would ask and five-year-old Jake in his chirpy voice, would answer, "Great, Opa", as they watched the Mets-Boston World Series game.

I last saw my father in April of 1988 in the hospital. His face was gaunt and yellow. His head, propped on a pillow, seemed too large for his body. He was now in a state of harmony, as he surrendered to my mother instead of arguing with her and allowed her to feed him. I had never seen such nurturing by my mom, nor such acceptance and appreciation from my father.

It was many months after his death that Jake suddenly burst into tears and felt the loss of his Opa, when his guinea pig, Bamba, died. It was the first time in his young life that he experienced loss. The guinea pig was his pathway to understanding what it meant to lose Opa, and he sobbed and asked questions about why people had to die, for months thereafter.

In contrast, I shed few tears and do not recall a deep sadness at the time of my father's death. In fact, it took me more 25 years before I visited his gravesite with my sister. In recent years certain emotions or actions that I take remind me of him, and I say, "He would have liked that", or I simply smile.

A short time after my father's death, my mother moved to Marja's apartment building. Marja lived a few floors above her, with her teenage son, Brian. Her devotion to our parents was always without question, and she had suggested that mommy should move closer to her.

They formed a symbiosis that worked for a while. Brian would eat dinners there when Marja came home late from work or would simply hang out or do his homework. I took my mom shopping and to doctor visits, and both Marja and I, effortlessly, formed the bridge between her and the outside world. Mom was included in all the normal planning that we both did. She was included in all holiday festivities, and when Sheila and I would vacation, she would come with us. Ironically, this woman who combined modernity and Victorian sensibilities, flowered after my father's death.

She could no longer rationalize a life put on hold because of my father's rigidity. Now she was pushed, pulled and supported with great empathy, by Marja, who would have made a gifted geriatric social worker. Her reverence for the aged, her patience and her matter of fact, hands-on approach helped my mother become a different person. Marja's tenacious efforts to empower our mother, a woman in her early eighties, resulted in many years of pleasure for her and everyone who knew her. Because mom started taking control of her life, she became pro-active. No longer would she wait for her son and daughter to call her or wait for them to invite her over.

The newfound energy boosted her self-esteem and gave her the determination a few years later to have hip replacement surgery, and then to travel to Europe with us. She met Tante Celine in Amsterdam and they traveled on their own to visit Oom Sam. It was as though she had lived in a thinly veiled cocoon for most of her adult life, and now was suddenly spreading her wings, flying into the daylight never to return to her previous stage. Here was a person who in some ways started life in her eighties and for the next 15 years aged extremely well, lived life to the fullest, and inspired all those around her.

At the same time, Sheila and I were hoping to have a second child. We had waited for almost six years, mostly because Sheila wasn't ready to have another child so soon. Beginnings inspired and exhausted her. A half a dozen miscarriages followed, numerous consultations with fertility specialists, and sperm count evaluations proved simply that the fertilized eggs were too old or no longer had the environment necessary to grow a healthy baby.

This period of six years was fraught with stress, sadness, frustration, and anger. The latter was not only evident in Sheila's anger towards herself, but my anger towards Sheila for not starting sooner. It was during that period, when Sheila was pregnant for the last time, that I prayed / begged God to support us in our quest for new life, but it was a prayer unfulfilled. Although adoption was discussed, we both felt overwhelmed by the process and less than ebullient going in that direction. As Sheila neared fifty, I suggested that we stop trying, not only because I feared that parenting would become much more physically demanding, but I believed that the quality of our retirement years would be undermined. The tension between us permeated the air and was inhaled by Jake.

He found it more and more difficult to confront me, and was overwhelmed by my anger, similar to my inability and fear of approaching my dad when he was angry. Sometimes words spewed out of my mouth like white volcanic ash, that sizzled and smoldered, sucking the oxygen out of the room.

In fact, Jake had night terrors and in his plea for help suggested that a hypnotist might solve his nightmares. Acknowledging his fear, we suggested that a therapist would be better. Surprised and saddened to hear of these night terrors, we hoped it would resolve itself. But, Jake was persistent about wanting help and kept asking if we had found a therapist.

He began seeing a wonderful therapist who met with us periodically and explained that his night terrors where related to the problems in our relationship. We were frequently angry with one another, snapping and arguing loudly. She suggested that we try couple therapy, which we did for several years and continued to do so whenever there were stresses that were better mediated by a therapist we both respected. Just as I needed a treehouse years before, Jake needed a safe space and a confidant. After a year of therapy, Jake's night terrors dissipated and our relationship was in a better place.

Whether it was because we had a son and a family, or the impact of my father's death, or the ongoing resentment I felt towards God and organized religion, our spiritual needs became more important, and we became more attentive to the recognition and celebration of certain Jewish holidays.

Spirituality, for me, is a feeling of sharing, of respect and a way of connecting. It is an oceanic feeling and it lives in my heart and mind. Rosh Hashanah, Hanukkah, Pesach, and the secular Thanksgiving became holidays that brought the inner sanctum together. Marja, her children, and eventually their respective spouses and children, Oma, Sheila's sister, Andrea, close friends and sometimes cousin Jack and Lucy, would attend. For Sheila and me this was a true blessing, because we observed these holidays from the center of our family home, rather than from a pew in a synagogue. We enjoyed the days of cooking, the various rituals, the dancing and singing while washing dishes after the meal, and a personalized Haggadah, developed and illustrated by Sheila.

We proudly saw ourselves as the ritual weavers, and as time went by, through mutual agreement, we parceled Hanukkah off to Steven and Brenda, and from time to time would celebrate July 4th or other holidays elsewhere.

It did not matter to us where it was held, just simply that the family looked forward to it and that it happened each year. The satisfaction derived from bringing family and friends together, for any purpose, with good food and drink, fed all the crevices of my being.

Playing the role of the patriarch, fulfilled me both as a man and as a father. Whether people viewed me that way or not didn't matter. In contrast to my father, I always wanted to play a central role in the family and, although Beit Hashita was a secular kibbutz, I remembered the pleasure I felt when participating in the Sukkot and Hanukkah festivals. We provided continuity and a sense of belonging to our gathered family.

I thought a lot about my past, my childhood, my erratic travels, contempt for organized religion, my reverence for life, and reaffirmed to myself what was truly important. How I conducted myself daily would be the hallmark of my religion.

Could I respect and tolerate ideas that were antithetical to my own, remain fair, empathic and consistent in my approach? These were the questions I asked myself and tenets that I tried to practice in the workplace, with friends and associates, but with less success at home. I behaved differently in public than in private. Somehow the home is a mirror of who you are, it reflects a quagmire of feelings, a past riddled with poor models, obscuring vision and objectivity and undermining civility itself. It took most of my life to narrow the credibility between my public and private persona, and this, still, remains an ongoing struggle.

I took up running, to reduce weight and perennial stress. Sometimes while running I would be deep in thought and forget that I was running at all. Some call this a runner's high, because it is an out-of-body experience. This would only happen when training for marathons, since my distances would increase from five to ten miles or more on any given run. Whether out of boredom or the humdrum of doing the same thing, my mind would wander and then fixate on a thought or picture. I would become unaware of my own motion, while remaining aware of my surroundings.

Training for a marathon required amazing discipline, energy, and vanity. It was an obsessive practice that came into my life during those days of relationship tension, when the best thing I could do was just, "Run, Joe, run!". The endorphins would kick in, the weight that I had gained after Jake was born was gone, I had more energy, and I sliced my tension in half.

The day of the NYC Marathon was a true people's celebration. I was not alone in feeling heroic, loved and applauded by a whole city. I ran the Marathon five times, with a friend, or by myself, and although I was never a fast runner, I always finished. Sheila and Jake would cheer me on in Brooklyn, and then take the train to Manhattan, walk to First Avenue to cheer once more, and then wait near the finish line in Central Park. The heavy medal slung from my neck and my thermal blanket, like a silvery cape, made me feel like an ancient Spartan coming home from battle.

The one negative about running a marathon was my theory about diet. I always ate robustly and felt that my marathon training would keep me in shape, which it did. But, I ate like that every-day of the year, while the training occurred for less than six months, resulting in a large weight fluctuation from one year to the next. Sadly, this false rational undermined my health a few years later.

31

My career was in full swing, Friends Seminary was celebrating its bicentennial and Beginnings was bursting at the seams. Jake was entering kindergarten at Friends, and the Chernobyl accident occurred. It was 1986. The sadness that followed had also stirred up enormous fears about potential nuclear disasters for people who lived near nuclear sites as in Pennsylvania and Long Island. While nearby municipalities updated their evacuation plans, I, in my absurdist humor, incorporated the word "Chernobyl" into Jake's bedtime routine.

Every night, Sheila or I read or made up a bedtime story for Jake, followed by a massage that I provided. When I told Jake to turn over and lay on his back, I would say, "Turnover Chernobyl". This routine lasted for several years and my comment was repeated over and over each night.

It was only many years later, when Jake understood what "Chernobyl" was, that he asked me about it. It was not my intention to make humor of the tragic event itself, or to be callous, but I have always used absurdist humor as a mechanism to undermine that which is sacred and to blunt the impact of horror.

For example, when friends recollected their joyful summer camp experiences and would ask me where I went, I would state (with a straight face), "That as a child, we summered in Dachau". Besides, "Turnover Chernobyl" had a nice ring to it.

The success of Beginnings and a stable job at Friends allowed Sheila and I to fantasize about owning a country home. From time to time we spent weekends in other people's homes and loved the respite from city life. It felt as though we were on vacation, far away from normal responsibilities, with endless open spaces, fields and lawns, trees, cows, cornfields and horse farms.

We would go berry picking, hiking, fishing, and lie under the clear, cool sky at night. We drew a circle around Manhattan with a radius of 150 miles, allowing us to look in NY, NJ, PA, CT, RI or MA. Our hope was to be no more than three hours from the city, to look primarily in the north, east or west and to be away from perceived resort attractions, such as beach or lakefront housing.

We primarily looked in the mid-Hudson counties of Greene and Columbia, which are on opposite sides of the Hudson River. The search for a home generated great anxiety. I worried about the cost and making the right decision. We had never had a mortgage, lived in a rent stabilized apartment, and the largest loan we had ever taken out was for a car of less than $6,000.

Our search was not very successful and just when we were about to purchase a house in Green County, our accountants made us aware that we were liable for substantial corporate and personal taxes, because of Beginnings' success. This meant that the money saved for the down payment went to the IRS and that ended our search.

In February 1988, we stayed for a weekend in a beautiful home in the town of Ancram, N.Y., surrounded by open rolling fields, barns, a pond, and snow. The old farmhouse had been restored to its original beauty, with a fireplace in the kitchen and living room, and many nooks and crannies typical of an 1850s home. Sheila sadly had the flu, but Jake and I had a grand time outdoors. When we thanked the owners for the weekend use of their home, we also asked if they knew of any "interesting" homes for sale.

A year later, Beverly (the same owner) called to let me know of a house in Columbia County that was owned by a Quaker institution. A Quaker foundation that helps provide housing in NYC, was deeded a home, plus acreage, that they were attempting to sell to the Audubon Society, without great luck.

When Sheila, Jake and I saw the property in February of 1989, we found a dark house that had not been lived in for several years, a corncrib that was clearly wracked, two barns, a silo, and tall sugar maples, bare to the branch. I loved the location and trees, but Sheila was appalled by the ugly 1950s renovation of the farmhouse interior, while Jake just moped around and said he didn't like it.

The mixed enthusiasm didn't stop me from finding the administrator of the Quaker foundation and much to my surprise, it was someone I knew. I was chagrined to find out that they had someone interested in the property and, also that the price was well beyond our capabilities. To make matters worse, I was still smarting from the sudden news of the tax liability and was a bit gun-shy about getting involved with another possible purchase.

By June I was told that the interested buyer was waiting for his own house to close and hoped to purchase the Foundation's property. Sheila and I went on vacation, mostly relieved that we hadn't waded into the real estate waters.

In August, while visiting Marja and Barbara, a close friend of hers who had rented a cabin in Gallatin, NY, I suggested that we go bowling, which Jake loved. The bowling lanes on route 9W were closed, and wouldn't reopen for two hours. I suggested that we go look at the Foundation's house again. Whereas Sheila saw it as a little adventure, Jake was resolutely against it because that would surely put an end to bowling.

With no GPS or any idea of the road names or the name of the town, we drove around Ancramdale. Suddenly, we realized that the property was right in front of us. Except, this time, there was foliage on the majestic maples, the two hydrangea trees were in full bloom and the house resting on a knoll, looked less dingy than before.

To our surprise there was a for sale sign on the lawn. The kitchen had been painted a soft yellow and Sheila found the house more appealing and had many ideas for restoration. Jake found a low hanging branch on a Norway maple to climb, and cows were mooing at us from across the road. The planets were aligned.

These were signs that this house was meant for us, and I was determined not to let it go again. Fortuitously, the original buyer had not been able to sell his own house, and backed out. At the same time the price had been reduced by more than 30%, because of the real estate market crash of 1989 when inflated prices spiraled downward.

Our mortgage search was a nightmare that truly tested our marriage. Sheila had recently suffered a miscarriage, was horribly depressed and in a state of total fatigue. We later found out that she was also anemic and the combination of the psychological and physical deterioration left her barely functioning. This added to my stress and swirled into a perfect storm that threw us out of rhythm.

In many ways, for me, the property represented a second child, but in significant ways it represented even more. To own land, to plant seeds, to form roots and to own a house, not only fulfilled the American immigrant dream, but provided such a sense of pride, peace and security that I would fight all the wind mills blocking my way to get the prize.

In my mind, I saw the property as a place that family and friends could share and hoped that it would become a family compound. Whereas the "negotiation" process with the Quaker administrator was both quick and civil, finding a bank willing to approve a mortgage was not. Our credit rating was marred by a single debt, of less than $100 that we paid two months late. There were many weeks of agony and strain.

Finally, a mortgage broker found a bank willing to offer us a mortgage. The closing occurred on a stormy day in November, and was over within less than a half an hour. Sheila and I were the only remaining people in the room, with our new keys and a white rabbit's foot, given to us by the mortgage broker.

During that first winter we were challenged by a number of incidents that were certainly new to our experience as city dwellers, although most likely common occurrences in old homes in rural areas. The live bat in our toilet, the large milk snake near an old radiator in the basement, the wood duck invasion and finding the cesspool plugged up and frozen, have all become part of our family folklore.

These incidents, however, were minor compared to the angst I felt every weekend before we arrived at our property. The "Copake Arsonist" was terrorizing the immediate area and periodically a barn or some commercial building was set ablaze. As we approached the small hill that blocked the view of our house, I feared that our barns would be ablaze or in charred ruins. I held my breath until we drove on top of the hill and saw our property as we had left it, perfectly intact. The anxiety I displayed was all too familiar, it was the fear that someone or something I love would be taken away from me and the sad confirmation that nothing stays permanent.

Over the years, we renovated the exterior of the house, added fire places, expanded the kitchen and dining area, and changed the farm basement into a multi-purpose space with darkroom, wine cellar, bathroom, bedrooms and exercise space.

My father would have loved the land. I often think of him, especially in the spring and summer when I am tilling the earth and tending to my vegetable garden. In fact, many years later we dedicated a memorial garden to both Yetta and Morris. We set aside an area on the highest point of the property, and housed beneath the grey gravel pebbles, green shrubbery and a few boulder-like rocks, lay Yetta's ashes and bottled earth from Morris's grave site.

Fortunately, my mom, who lived until 2003, appreciated the property and spent July and holiday periods with us each year in the country. Every summer, she sat on the wooden porch with her big floppy canvas hat, culottes pants, bold print cotton blouse and a glass of hot tea, doing her crossword puzzles. Sometimes, she would look up, take a deep breath and look at the fields and orchard, and then return to her crossword.

The property which we planned to call "Een Klein Beetje", or "a little bit", became a center for family and friends. Jake's "secular" Bar Mitzvah, or as he liked to call it, his "fake" Bar Mitzvah, and his annual reunion of college and high school friends, took place at our Ancramdale property. It became the site for the annual celebration of religious and secular holidays. Its location was perfect, because it was three hours from Boston, two plus hours from NYC, an hour plus from Albany, and most importantly, twenty minutes from both Massachusetts and Connecticut.

To me, psychologically, it served as my precious space, the center of the layered onion, the place to go to, when climate change floods the coastal cities. It will be Noah's Ark and terra firma. It was also a sign that I had made it, a status symbol for sure, a luxury, and thus a black hole as well.

The property also brought Jake and his Oma Yetta closer together.

She was the perfect companion and partner, especially during his pre-teen years, when she taught him how to play Gin Rummy. They played endlessly, kept score, and talked about their lives, sang together and told each other silly jokes.

Every so often, she would slip him a five or a ten-dollar bill, and he, dutifully, would add half to his savings and buy some comic books or baseball cards with the other half. Without her guidance and support, his country experience would have been much diminished.

Years later, when Jake became older, they switched roles, and he became the guide and partner for her. She was 90, slowing down, and looked forward to the card games and loving attention he provided. His tales were active and stimulating and wrapped around dates and girlfriends, playing baseball, college and work. In fact, one of Jake's college entry essays revolved around his experiences with his Oma as he grew up, and the dynamic of being guided by her in his youth and the reversal as she aged.

I watched their interactions over that long span with immense pleasure and more than a pinch of envy, since I never met my own grandparents. I always had great reverence for the elderly, especially my parents, who I always viewed as old, and I devoted my time and effort to their wellbeing. I was glad to witness my son foster a similar sentiment towards his Oma, and, in a subtle way, hoped that as I aged, he would pay homage to me as well.

32

In 1991, the first Hidden Child conference was held in NYC. I attended with Marja and Sheila, Jack and Jack's wife, Lucy. I had not thought about my fragile beginnings in more than ten years, and in some ways, was annoyed to face them again, head on. The gathering at the Marriott Hotel brought together over 1600 people, who were mostly in their fifties and sixties. Many had never spoken of their experience in public and in some cases even their respective families didn't know their stories.

I came to the conference with definite ambivalence, while Marja hoped to gain recognition and confirmation for her life's angst that was related to the war. Although born six months after the war, she absorbed *in utero* the fear, anxiety and loss that my mother experienced. As a young child, she inhaled the stress and sadness they lived with every day.

I recall Marja fervently looking for workshops that dealt with the impact of WWII on children born at war's end. She couldn't find any and felt angry that her trauma was not recognized. Twenty-five years later, in 2016, children who were *in utero* during the war were finally recognized as victims and eligible to receive war reparation money.

Sheila attended the conference to support me and learn more about my experiences as a hidden child. There were workshops, a movie and some speakers that few people listened to because they were much more interested in listening to each other's stories. There had never been a forum for hidden children to share their stories, and it served as a catharsis for many people.

For me the conference forced me to look at my past, to listen to other peoples' stories and experiences and through subsequent meetings to understand how our stormy beginnings impacted us as adults. More importantly, I reasoned that such an experience can either diminish who you are or strengthen you. I chose the latter.

What I appreciated most about the conference was that it inspired many small group discussions afterwards at people's homes. I joined a group in lower Manhattan and found that most of the attendees were from Eastern Europe and mostly female, possibly because men are generally less comfortable sharing their feelings in group settings.

I attended many meetings and even had a retreat with my group at our country home. I hadn't realized until then that more male children were killed because they were circumcised and more easily found out. I also inferred that life for the persecuted in Poland and most Eastern European countries was often worse than the plight of Jewish children in western European countries.

For some, the scars of war were further deepened by the fact that they were placed in camps for displaced people after the war ended. These wretched camps that were organized to make sense out of chaos, in some cases persisted until the mid-1950s.

I also realized that I was younger than most of the group members and my innocence protected me from vestiges of psychological harm that plagued many of the others. Although we were all damaged in some way, mostly having to do with issues of trust, we somehow managed to carve out a life for ourselves and in many cases a successful one.

Our group of twelve was equally divided between people who in some way were still mourning their lost families and lost childhoods, and others who refused to look at the past and only faced forward. One other Dutch survivor and I seemed to reflect the attributes of both groups. I think that was because our experiences were not as harsh as those faced by many Eastern European children.

Some, who were separated from their parents, at age seven or eight, had hid on their own, while others at a younger age were converted into Christianity (for their protection) and didn't find out about their past until they were in their twenties.

For two women, the war didn't end until the early 1950s, when the displacement camps were shut down and they made their way to the States.

There was no doubt that we were all survivors, who had adapted and who would continue to adapt to new circumstances. We would bend but not break. The question was, could we truly thrive, let go and be happy? That might not happen, or in any case, had not happened yet. After a few years, the group disbursed. I lost track of most of the members, but continued to attend some of the International Hidden Child conferences.

The Conference reconnected me with several members of my family, especially Jack and Lucy, and my cousin, Janneke Trompetter Dazzo, who was about eight years older than me and lived in California. It also inspired a family reunion of the Trompetter and Gosler households living in the US and abroad. Family members came from California, Florida, Delaware, Pennsylvania, New England, and Holland.

Our country house served as the center for the reunion, where some festivities were held and several people were housed. Most of the gathered stayed in nearby inns and small hotels. Although I felt that I always needed to have one foot out the door, for fear of being physically, emotionally, or socially caught in a web from which I couldn't escape, I loved the reunion, and like a honeybee would meander from one person to another.

33

By 1992, I was still at Friends Seminary and in the middle of my third five-year plan. When I was in my early twenties I devised a simple philosophy related to work. If I couldn't bicycle to work, I wouldn't take the job, and that a term of work should not exceed five years. I believed that if you wanted to do well it should be achievable within five years. Besides, the world was expansive and ever changing and I didn't want to get stuck in a dead-end job. I stayed true to this philosophy until I was in my mid-thirties and then, without hesitation, forgot all about it.

Twelve years had passed and I was happy to continue at Friends for a while longer. But, since I always looked ten years back and ten years forward, the question was, where would I want to be in ten years. The more I pondered that question the more I thought about retirement and the possibility of trying other things.

I met with a financial planner, who asked me to outline my vision for retired life, including what I planned to do and what resources I would need for it to become a reality. We met again a few weeks later, and I blurted out that I would like my retirement to begin when I was in my mid-fifties. He said that it was possible, but that I would have to scale down my vision quite a bit, and probably work half time. That didn't sound like a good plan at all, and so I went back to the drawing board.

In some ways, I felt as though I was negotiating a deal for our lives with a financial planner who felt like a medium between myself and an invisible future force. After thinking it over and discussing it with Sheila, I met with the planner one more time. I proposed retiring at 62 and selling Beginnings. The planner went through his calculator and horoscope, and responded positively, "That's a plan!"

Within a few years thereafter, the glow of my planned retirement was replaced by disillusionment. Was it the length of time until retirement, or my restlessness at work, or what might be called a mid-life crisis? Whatever it was, it clung to me, like a dampness on my bones. I was gaining weight and seemed more stressed than I had been for quite a while.

I had ambivalence about running another marathon. I had run five and this annual NYC celebration no longer enticed me as in previous years. Besides, Sheila no longer came to cheer, and Jake was turning fourteen and had other things to do, like being a teenager. Yet, I pushed myself to do it again. Why? What would happen if I decided not to do it one year, or not to do it ever again? Would my spirit die; would I be less than I am?

I had run the marathon numerous times and somehow the discipline of following through was ultra-important to me. I took pride in this discipline. It reminded me of the persistence my father showed whenever he needed to repair something or complete a project. He would become obsessed and jump through hoops and fire to finish what he had promised to himself or others. That single-mindedness, that some would call rigidity and others would admire, had its ugly side as well.

It came as no surprise to me, Marja or my mother, when poppy would find himself emotionally boxed in by one chore or another. His voice then exploded in anger as he paced back and forth, like an animal trapped in a cage.

I carried my stress differently, in my shoulders, my chest and my lower back. I had learned enough about myself so that my outbursts were now less frequent, though they were still directed at my loved ones.

That said, I accumulated stress in the same manner that I accumulated weight. I neither understood why I was tense nor how to make it disappear. No doubt my erratic training contributed to my weight gain. My ambivalence about running another marathon influenced the distance, pace and number of times I ran each week. I ran less and more slowly than other training years, possibly because of my added weight and getting older. I do know I was very angry at a fellow worker.

I felt tormented by a fellow worker, who accused me of not paying tuition for my son's enrollment at the school. This employee had a chip on his shoulder to begin with and was chronically late. As his supervisor, I told him that this would no longer be tolerated.

At the same time, I was very upset that he was questioning my honesty, given that the trait of honesty was central to my core. His comments made me feel threatened because periodically I used Friends' stamp machine to mail out Beginnings' monthly billing statements. I had paid all of it back, but remained guilt-ridden about misusing employer property for my own purposes. I intertwined that guilt with the employee accusation.

Similarly, I hated the annual audit process, when field auditors and senior auditors came to review the annual financial operations of the School. Everything was attended to in the most ethical and professional manner, but the simple scrutiny by these accountants irrationally reminded me of the Gestapo.

The anxiety within me sometimes surfaced in the form of sweat, or a tight chest, or a knot in the pit of my stomach. My fear of being "found out", of being different than I appeared to be and less competent, was irrational and in essence, I was reliving my parents' nightmare. For them being found out meant certain death—for me it meant total loss of self. My stress was not relieved until the annual audit blood-letting was over.

The cool October air brushed against my cheeks and felt invigorating as I ran past the wetlands and down Crest Lane. Sheila had decided to stay in the city to attend an enrollment fair and to visit a friend in the hospital. I decided to take Jake, the laundry and our cat, Tina, upstate for the weekend. I was surprised by how much energy I had during my run, given the lavish meal I had the night before.

Once a week at our favorite restaurant, I would treat myself to an appetizer of snails baked in brie, butter and garlic, a rack of lamb with roasted potatoes, fortified by wine, coffee and dessert. The marathon was three weeks away and this was my last long run.

I was returning to the house, when I felt a flutter-like sensation across my chest. Was it the wind ruffling my T-shirt? I didn't care. I was happy that I had just finished a sixteen-mile run and triumphantly went into the house to stretch. I sat down on the kitchen bench, taking a minute's rest before I would begin to stretch on the floor, as I always did after a run. I heard the phone ring, but I was nowhere near it. I had blacked out. I was on the floor looking up and Jake was coming down the stairs. "Hello mom", Jake said into the phone, "Pop's on the floor. I think he's stretching? Do you want to talk to him?" "Pop, mom wants to talk to you."

With impeccable timing, Sheila had a premonition that there was something wrong, and called just when I blacked out. I got up slowly, the way a boxer would after the count of eight, and picked up the phone. "Are you alright?" Sheila asked. "I don't know", I answered. I proceeded to tell her that the last thing I remembered was sitting on the bench and then finding myself on the floor.

Clearly, I had fainted, and, whether out of fear, shock, or disrupting my normal Sunday routine, I didn't want to give it credence and dismissed it as insignificant. I simply wanted to pack up and drive Jake and Tina back to the city, and deal with it on Monday.

An argument ensued, and I stubbornly wouldn't listen to Sheila's concern and logic. In desperation, she called Marja, who also battered me with her concern and began to wear down my resistance. I finally agreed to take my fainting seriously when Sheila said to me, "Do you want to put Jake's life at risk by driving back to the city?" I packed the car with Jake and Tina and drove to Sharon Hospital.

"Your heart enzymes are off the chart", the doctor stated after perusing the EKG and blood test results, "but that can also be caused by your long run." By this time, Sheila and Marja were at the hospital. The definitive pronouncement of a mild heart attack was a shock.

I had always had vested interest in exhibiting myself as a pillar of health and fortress of impregnability especially to Jake. My sudden vulnerability and possible death hit Jake hard and cracked the invulnerable image he carried of me.

Excusing himself from the hospital room, he went to the bathroom and silently cried his fears out. For years thereafter, Jake was very careful not to upset me for fear that it would cause another heart attack. No doubt it impacted his own teen development. Sheila was also shocked and feared that I might die. For Jake, Sheila, Marja and me, it took several years of living to calm us down and return to a normal relationship and steady family rhythm.

I stayed at Sharon Hospital for several days, and was then taken by ambulance all the way to Manhattan, to NYU Medical Center.

Two days later, I was wheeled into the operating room where an angiogram was taken, followed by angioplasty.

Although I was immobilized after being sedated, I had not yet lost consciousness and recalled the doctor and his assistants talking about a great Chinese restaurant. Somehow, I was not pleased to hear them talk about such frivolous matters, as I faded into unconsciousness.

"You have three stents in you", the nurse said with a smile, suggesting I should feel as proud as an infantryman who had just become a three-star general. An hour or two thereafter, two young doctors looked at my hip area, where the catheter had been inserted, and proceeded to do something directly out of medieval medical ritual. They took out the catheter and proceeded to press on my hip area for about twenty minutes until they were confident that the bleeding had stopped. I was amused by the incongruity of a late 20th-century delicate procedure called angioplasty and the strong hands of two male doctors applying pressure to the incision. It was a painful but necessary completion of angioplasty.

My mild heart attack resulted in some scarring under my heart and a total blockage of the right coronary artery, which was the reason I fainted. "Thank God this happened during a training run", Sheila said, since she knew I would never have stopped midway during the marathon, and could have died.

The "tap" on the shoulder, as I called it some years later, profoundly changed my life. I was happy to go home, where I would have all of Sheila and Jake's attention. I was in a daze, grey in color and felt jolted like the headpin after being hit by a bowling ball on its way towards a "strike".

The "tap" made me aware of my mortality and pushed me to re-evaluate my life. I did an actuarial inventory: what made me tense, what gave me joy and so on. I realized, if only mechanically, I would have to overhaul my diet, stop skipping breakfast, and review my approach to work and responsibilities in general.

I bemoaned that I could no longer eat my favorite rack of lamb and cried the first time I witnessed someone else eating it at my favorite restaurant. "I am not going to eat rabbit food", I said to Sheila as we walked out of the restaurant, knowing full well that I had to radically change my diet.

The impact of my heart attack directly influenced what we ate. Since I did most of the day-to-day cooking, that meant that our diet as a family had to change: Butter, sugar, fat and many white starches were eliminated as were many dairy products.

Sheila cornered the market on fat-free cookbooks. I experimented with pizza dough made with beer, meatless lasagna, egg whites and "fake" fat-free cheese that I called "DuPont cheese" because of its synthetic composition.

Sheila and Jake didn't look forward to my dinners with the same expectation and joy they had previously shown. Sheila, who loves to bake, experimented with fat-free baking, most of which ended up in the garbage.

More profoundly, I continued to worry about the impact my heart attack had on Jake. After all, I always maintained a façade of one who got things done, someone who was never sick or late for work. Was this yet another mask, like 20 years before, that needed to be cast aside or broken? What shocks, what doubt and self-doubt did Jake experience, witnessing me change from being indestructible to someone who was vulnerable?

Upon reflection, Jake went through the expected teen evolution vis-à-vis Sheila, where he either avoided her, or they locked horns, but he didn't do it with me. Could it be the tap on the shoulder that undermined his will and spirit, to act out towards me during his teen years, or was it his memory of my experience as a hidden child? Either event could have easily stunted this caterpillar from gaining wings. Fortunately, Sheila knew me better than I knew myself, understanding the vicissitudes of life and paid closer attention to me than before, as we would for each other and helped me through this sobering time.

It was also the first time in my life that I had to take prescription drugs. They made me urinate more often, strained my muscles and limbs, and undermined my sex drive. Thankfully, Viagra, the little blue pill, helped me with the latter, but the dependency on drugs to continue living well made me feel even more vulnerable.

Ultimately, the dependence on these drugs, the doctor visits that followed, traumatic health experiences that occurred to friends and colleagues, forced me to listen to my body for the first time.

I was no longer a slave to time. Sometimes I was late and other times I would skip meetings altogether. Flexibility and adaptation, hallmarks of my management approach, but not my lifestyle, became more a part of my everyday life. No longer, like the marathoner, would I force my way through the runner's wall, coming through the other side, heroic, but diminished. I avoided that challenge altogether. As the saying goes: "You don't have to be shot at to know that it is bad for you".

A year after my heart attack, the scars beneath my heart were gone, and I continued my journey, knowing I was on the right path.

34

As I watched my son grow older and more competent, I realized that it would be best to stay out of his way, and maybe, learn to let go as well. I think if my past had been more stable and less transient, with supportive parents and deep roots in the community, my approach to parenting would have been much less obsessive. The latter was difficult to do, given my own "fatherless" upbringing.

In any case, I felt more and more assured that Jake could solve his own problems. He cultivated an intimacy with friends in such a way that some filled the role of the siblings he never had. This sense that he could take care of himself, and that through friendship he had created an extended family, gave me great confidence in him.

Flying, which had always been an anxiety-filled experience, now became less so. Although flight, in every sense of that word, had always been a nerve-racking experience, it was compounded when Jake was born.

The knowledge that he had become a mensch and was capable of living in the world gave me immense solace and made me less anxious.

I was also cognizant that Jake was midway through high school. I did not look forward to that day when he would leave and follow his own path, wherever it led him, and I began to mourn my loss well before he graduated. In fact, I thought, half-jokingly that maybe I should take a job as the manager of some motel near Jake's future college.

It reminded me of the time, ten years earlier when I followed Jake as he marched to school on his own for the first time. Sheila found my reaction somewhat amusing, but understood that it would take a long time for new feelings and expectations to percolate through me before I was willing to accept them.

My relationship with Jake is not without bumps and bruises but has the potential for growth. On the other hand, my relationship with Marja is tenuous. Whether it's related to my economic ascent, my stubbornness and arrogance, or the historical dynamic between us, I am not sure.

For years, there were skirmishes and loud arguments, sometimes followed by crying, sometimes by phone disconnects, leaving both of us emotionally bruised and scarred. We would never be mistaken for twins, but in many ways, we are joined at the hip.

Besides a physical resemblance, we share the same fountain of anger, the same sense of burden, love for family and the nurturing of life itself. Yet, we are very different.

For a while, at least in our youth, I could do no wrong in her eyes. This changed by the mid-eighties. Whether it was a need to carve out her own identity, her struggles as a single parent, her sense of deprivation, or my arrogance and unwillingness to recognize her as a person of worth, our clashes escalated.

Although we love each other dearly and always support each other in times of need, we operate best at a safe distance. The wounds of childhood never fully heal. The time has passed to ask who's to blame, or how can we remedy this sad dynamic. It is time to accept that this is the way it is and hope that it is sustainable for the future.

Beginnings was now an established school, with a stellar reputation and more than 140 part-time students and a staff of 20. We even had some teenage "alumni" who volunteered in the summer program. Years thereafter, these same volunteers became parents and sent their own children to the school.

In fact, it was no longer Sheila's school, or playpen; it had a legacy and had taken on a life of its own. The knowledge that Sheila could retire, and that we could sell the school without it losing its luster, was a revelation. It formed the foundation of our retirement plans and gave us hope that things would work out financially.

We were deep into our empire-building phase of life, with a new Volvo, that we named Velma (it was fun and absurd to give names to everyday inanimate objects). We were planning for Jake's college and our own retirement, adding a pool and orchard to our country home, and annually traveling to the Caribbean. The years of sacrifice, and 12-hour-work days had brought us to this new landscape of opportunity and opulence.

Concurrently, I became less and less enthused by my work. Whether transfixed by Beginnings' success, planning for retirement or preoccupied with the responsibilities and challenges of my job, I was no longer stimulated by work and ambition was no longer the pied piper that urged me on. The fallout from what became day-to-day drudgery felt like dust clouding my spirit.

I knew that it was time to move on, but where? I had been working at Friends for over 17 years, and I knew that I would never want to work anywhere else. Given our grand plan it was too early to retire.

The question is what should I do now? I have no luxury of time, to retrace my steps, to find a different outcome. Nor do I want to rest on the feathery pillow of one's laurels. Would I get bitter and feel enslaved, stuck in the job, as I did over 30 years before? To mitigate those feelings, I started to take on new projects.

Not only was I coaching middle school baseball, which gave me immense pleasure, but my outside trusteeships and NYSAIS related Business Affairs work breathed new life into my fading spirit. The allowance of time to participate in other endeavors, would not have been possible without Rich Eldridge, the Principal. He understood the value of self-actualization, of encouraging employees' growth in personal matters of interest. I felt rejuvenated. I created a bridge to my future and I was in control of my fate.

CLOSING

The 2003-2004 school year was the year of my retirement. It was a surprisingly stress-free year, in part because it was my last year, and I was not responsible for the yearly audit. The administration and the school community feted me and celebrated my passage from an employee to an esteemed alum in meaningful ways.

Fulfilling my fantasy of cooking and serving the Friends' community in the school cafeteria, was a highlight of my last days at the school. There were other such moments and days, and Donna, the Director of Development, and her team's creativity and care in planning my retirement party went well beyond my expectations. I felt truly loved!

The pleasure and excitement of retirement was marred by the death of four women. Icons who represented the past and changed my familial landscape. These matriarchs were the center of their respective nuclear families. They were the ritual makers, the communicators within and amongst the families and caretakers of memory through word and photo. They held everything together!

My mother died just after Thanksgiving in 2003, with Tante

Celine and Tante Rosette Trompetter and Sara Wolper (Sheila's mom) all passing within 12 months of one another. Thankfully, they did not die prematurely. Sara was 87, and my mom and aunts were well into their nineties.

Marja, Sheila and I spent the last week of my mother's life at her bedside. For her grandchildren, she propped herself up, asked lucid questions and regaled them with her humor. As soon as they left, she slid down on the bed, rolled on her side, closed her eyes, maintained a fetal position and returned to the moaning she engaged in before they arrived. Her kidneys were failing, but Yetta was not going to be hurried or consoled into "letting go". She wanted to live until no breath came forward.

The passing of these matriarchs created a subtle ripple effect on all the remaining family members. Years before, their children—essentially a group of cousins—took on the responsibility of marking and celebrating the various religious holidays and familial traditions.

But now we understood, soberly, that our parents were no longer the custodians of the past. There was a subtle shift—like a continental drift—that made me, Marja, Sheila, Marion, Jimmy and Jack, the new elders and the keepers of family memory.

When the matriarchs died, we became the old ones and, like an heirloom hidden in a precious wooden chest, that reverence was transferred to us. The role of the elder is familiar to me. In fact, in some ways I've been old since childhood. It is neither a badge of honor nor something to bemoan, it just is.

PHOTOS

To seek refuge from the daily brutality of war, my
father took up drawing.

The family Dijkstra house in Wageningen where I was hidden.

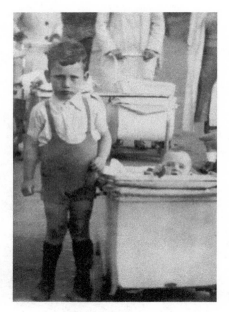

Groningen, me and Marja, 1946.

Me celebrating VE Day, about 1948.

Me, at home, on the kibbutz.

Israel, a class trip to the beach.

Late 1953, before our voyage to America: left to right, Marion, Rosie, Johnnie, me, Marja, Tante Emmy, two friends, and my parents.

The SS Constitution arriving in NYC harbor, 1953: Assorted people including Marja, Marion and my parents.

Rockaway Park, 1954: Johnny, Rosie, Marja, Marion
and me.

Poppy and his Buick.

Moeder Dijkstra.

Vader Dijkstra.

Anneke Dijkstra.

Folie Dijkstra

The Netherlands, 1963, me and cousin Andy.

Maine, cousin Jack and me.

Morocco, 1972, me, Sheila and Gopher.

Groningen, early 1970s: me, mommy and nephew
Steven.

Nephews Brian and Steven, about 1980.

A family celebration: left to right, Sheila, Marja,
mommy, poppy and me.

Our son, Jake, at age two.

Sheila, 1988.

Jake and me, 1994.

Milton and our house.

EPILOGUE

It was a Saturday morning in February 2007. Layers of snow covered the fields, white without a hint of green. Everything was clear and expectant. We were on a mission to pick up our puppy, Milton, from the breeder. Fortified with an old towel and a pet carrier, he sat on Sheila's lap in the car, whimpering and yelping, a blond, furry butterball. He would fill our empty nest and most profoundly link me to my past and create meaningful routines in the present. Now, retired, I could walk Milton three times a day, bathing in the adoration shown to him by strangers. The walks made me feel more alive and visible.

It was easy to make space for him in our hearts and he became an important member of our family. Milton's addition to our nest not only grounded me, but created a daily rhythm whose sweet and soothing vibrations reminded me of different periods in my life that were filled with excitement and slivers of hope, even though sadness and anxiety were always lurking beneath the surface. Though I still have dreams that can unsettle me, my days are filled with small and large projects that please me and I sleep well at night.

Eleven years later we mourned Milton's death, and yet I knew I had space in my heart for one more dog. In May of 2018, we brought home Reuben, a near-white plump furry puppy. Although he licked us profusely as Milton did, he also gave us little love bites from time to time. This alone should have warned us that Reuben was going to be very different from Milton.

Today, at ten months, he weighs 65 pounds, is very strong, willful and playful, and is still growing. As a hyper pup, he playfully jumps on people, pulls on his leash and likes to wrap his canine teeth around my wrist. Suffice it to say he's quite a challenge. In fact, in contrast, Milton has now been canonized Saint Milton.

Reuben is a smart dog, but has a healthy lab's skepticism and seems to question everything that's asked of him. He's a work in progress. I love him because he's not a clone, he's not like any other dog, has a strong personality and is determined to live robustly and enjoy the world around him.

I too am committed to living fully and enjoying the world around me, made richer by his presence. Like Reuben, I am still a work in progress and thankfully will continue in that state indefinitely.

Reuben's singularity reminds me that we are all unique and irreplaceable. Should we not embrace, or at least tolerate that which is different? Though challenging at times, our differences are the very core that extends our lives and makes us richer.

And so, I continue to walk my dog, have a reverence for life and the living, cultivate my garden and follow my moral compass.

ABOUT THE AUTHOR

Joseph Gosler was born in Groningen, the Netherlands during WWII and after the war he migrated to Israel with his family and subsequently to the United States, where he has lived since. His life's journey has been a circuitous one and as a result he has often meandered off the main road. This is best exemplified by the 20 plus years it took him to achieve his BA in History and MBA in corporate finance through the City University of New York.

For nearly 40 years he has worked in educational settings ranging from day care centers to private schools in the capacity of Business Manager. He and his wife founded a pre-school called Beginnings Nursery, have one son and live in New York City.

Mr. Gosler retired from Friends Seminary in 2004, and today is actively involved in several Quaker projects, writing, gardening, traveling and walking his dog. *Searching for Home*, describing his life as a Hidden Child, is his international debut.